THE
WORLD CRISIS
AND BIBLE PROPHECIES

DISCERNING THE SIGNS OF
THE LATTER DAYS

DR. HECTOR CARAM-ANDRUET

CREATION
HOUSE

THE WORLD CRISIS AND BIBLE PROPHECIES
by Dr. Hector Caram-Andruet
Published by Creation House
A Charisma Media Company
600 Rinehart Road
Lake Mary, Florida 32746
www.charismamedia.com

This book or parts thereof may not be reproduced in any form, stored in a retrieval system, or transmitted in any form by any means—electronic, mechanical, photocopy, recording, or otherwise—without prior written permission of the publisher, except as provided by United States of America copyright law.

Unless otherwise noted, all Scripture quotations are from the New American Standard Bible—Updated Edition, Copyright © 1960, 1962, 1963, 1968, 1971, 1972, 1973, 1975, 1977, 1995 by The Lockman Foundation. Used by permission. (www.Lockman.org)

Scripture quotations marked NKJV are from the New King James Version of the Bible. Copyright © 1979, 1980, 1982 by Thomas Nelson, Inc., publishers. Used by permission.

Design Director: Bill Johnson
Cover design by Justin Evans

Copyright © 2014 by Dr. Hector Caram-Andruet
All rights reserved.

Library of Congress Cataloging-in-Publication Data: 2013957290
International Standard Book Number: 978-1-62136-728-4
E-book International Standard Book Number: 978-1-62136-727-7

While the author has made every effort to provide accurate telephone numbers and Internet addresses at the time of publication, neither the publisher nor the author assumes any responsibility for errors or for changes that occur after publication.

First edition

14 15 16 17 18 — 9 8 7 6 5 4 3 2 1
Printed in Canada

DEDICATION

To the Holy Spirit of God,

who guided me through the
writing of this book.

To my wife, Grace; my children,
Martin, Roger, and Andrea;

and my grandchildren, Ian and Lucas.

CONTENTS

Preface 1
The World Crisis and Its Spiritual Significance 3
Warnings 10
- What Is a Warning? 10
- Spiritual Warnings 12

Spiritual Signs 18
- What Is a Spiritual Sign? 18
- The Greatest Spiritual Sign 19
- Hatred and Evil 23
- Spiritual Signs of Jesus' Coming 27

External Signs 41
- Signs Already Occurred 41
  - Return of the Jewish People to the Promised Land 41
  - Jerusalem Repossessed 42
  - The Flourishing of Israel 46
- Signs of the Latter Days 47
  - Knowledge Will Increase 47
  - Warfare of the Mind 49
  - The Surge of Emotionality vs. Spirituality 53
  - The Constraining of Freedom 60
  - The Manipulation of Fear 65

The Latter Days and Events to Follow 69
- Chronology of Events 70
- The Rapture 70
- The Removal of the Constrainer 76
- The Great Tribulation Period 77
  - The Antichrist and the False Prophet 78
    - Peace Treaty with Israel 80
    - The Rebuilding of the Temple 80
    - The Ten Kingdoms 81

- The Judgments of God 81
  - The Seven Seals 82
  - The 144,000 Jewish Preachers 84
  - The Casting of Satan from Heaven 85
  - The Antichrist Breaks His Covenant with Israel 86
  - Gog and Magog Invade Israel 86
  - The Antichrist Occupation of Palestine 90
  - The Antichrist's False Death 90
  - The Abomination of Desolation 91
  - The Antichrist Will Rule the World 92
  - The Two Witnesses 95
  - Babylon 99
    - Spiritual Babylon 99
    - Political, Economic, and Commercial Babylon 102
  - The Seven Trumpets 105
  - The Seven Bowls 107
- The War of Armageddon 113
- The Second Coming 116
- The Millennium 120
- Merger of the Millennium Kingdom with the Eternal Kingdom of God 135
- The Great White Throne 135
- The Creation of a New Heaven and a New Earth 137
- Eternity 140
  - Kinship with God 140
  - Fellowship with God 141
  - Coheirs with Christ 141
  - A Kingdom of Peace 141
  - A Kingdom of Virtue 142
  - A Kingdom of Joy 142

- A Kingdom Without Trials 142
- A Kingdom of Glory 143

Conclusions and Admonishments 144
- Conclusions 144
  - On the World Crisis 145
  - On Spiritual Warnings 149
  - On Spiritual Signs 150
  - On External Signs 151
  - On Latter-Days Events 153
- Admonishments 158
  - We Need God's Help 158
  - Do Not Be Proud 159
  - Open the Door of Your Heart 159
  - Reject Temptation 160
  - Follow His Lead 161
  - Keep His Commandments 161
  - Talk to God 162
  - Have a Personal Relationship with God ... 164

A Personal Note from the Author 165
Notes 166

PREFACE

THIS BOOK IS addressed to all men, Christians and non-Christians, who may be led by the Spirit of God to read it—to the former, for spiritual edification; to the latter, hopefully for salvation.

It has been written and structured giving full preeminence to the Word of God, seeking the leading and guidance of the Holy Spirit in the comments and interpretations interwoven with it. Latter-days prophecies are complex and profound and pose a great responsibility for the Bible interpreter. For this reason the author has depended intensely on the guidance of the Spirit and has scarcely resorted to bibliography on the subject, instead relying on the extensive use of concordances and historical references.

The style used by the author, with captioned paragraphs and sub-paragraphs, seeks clarity for the readers, while the text of selected scriptures and concordances are fully incorporated to facilitate its reading and interpretation.

The underlying problem with certain Bible doctrines and their exponents lies in the manner of interpretation. The author supports the literal interpretation of the Scriptures, which was the position of the early church. This does not deny the need for discernment—being a precious gift of the Spirit—but it does emphatically oppose the adding to or taking away from the Word, as the Lord has solemnly warned us (Rev. 22:18–19).

For consistency reasons, the New Standard American Bible has been used, and all Scripture quotes are written in italic font.

Chapter 1

THE WORLD CRISIS AND ITS SPIRITUAL SIGNIFICANCE

THE WORLD IS going through a crisis like it has never experienced before. Notice that I am not only referring to the world economic recessionary trends afflicting various international markets, such as the service, industrial, and commercial sectors. I am not just addressing the nearly collapsing financial system, as reflected by unstable international stock markets, the banking system, the instability of most major currencies and commodities. I am neither singularizing the astonishing levels of public and private debt and unprecedented public deficit conditions in advanced countries, as well as emerging ones. Nor am I referring to "virtual" financial instruments like derivatives, whose monetary significance is estimated at over four hundred trillion US dollars (or over twenty-five times the gross national product of the United States of America) and whose trading mechanisms are virtually unregulated.

I am, however, raising as a concern that outside the inner circles of power (and I will later in this book expand on what is actually behind all this), the true significance of what is going on is not being accurately communicated or understood by most people around the world. Even uncontaminated and non-manipulated economists, financial experts, and specialized reporters restrain their opinions and limit their counseling in terms of scope and time. This is not only so because of erratic and unstable overall conditions but also because it is politically and professionally unwise to venture beyond certain boundaries.

World affairs, like never before in recent history, are presently controlled by international interest groups whose power goes beyond governments and institutions and that manipulate global economic and financial trends through interwoven banking networks. These groups also control the price and availability of major commodities such as oil and gold and extend their power into money laundering, drug and armament trafficking, and the value of international currencies. Needless to say, these groups have a decisive influence on international policies and affairs. They promote large-sized government structures as a means to exercise easier control, to manipulate, and to corrupt.

During periods of profound change, the real difficulty lies in discerning between causes and effects. As an example, consider public spending by governments beyond Congress' approved national budgets, resulting in significant annual deficits. Has this been caused by political reasons, by indiscipline, by incompetence, by corruption, in response to national security objectives (a conveniently broad concept), or to stimulate the economies and sustain consumption, to name some of the most used justifications? The solutions attempted to solve fiscal deficits, such as increased taxation; the downward manipulation the interest rates paid to the money-saving populations (taking wealth away from them, as a hidden tax); and reducing investments in critical areas such as education, technological development, and the countries' infra-structures, roads and public transportation, are actually harming nations rather than providing solutions. This occurs while inefficiency, low productivity, and excessive spending—the true causes of fiscal deficits—remain unattended. Further, because some of those measures are politically unpopular, the easy way out over the short term is for central banks to print money, which inevitably leads to inflation over the medium and long terms and which represents the worst economic calamity that countries can encounter. This is so because while inflation erodes the purchasing power of the entire population, it especially affects the lower socio-economic levels of society, who are more dependent on the prices of such essential items like food, medicine, fuel, and basic services.

The same could be said about stimulating consumption beyond a reasonable and sustainable level of personal income, as it is presently happening in many nations via monetary stimulus policies, low-equity mortgage loans, unrestrained leasing and loan facilities, low interest rates, and the unchecked use of credit cards, to name a few examples. All of this is encouraged by governments themselves to keep the economies from recessing and by the private sector via commercial advertising and promotions aimed at fomenting fictitious lifestyles. Such policies are unsustainable and will inevitably result in the tragedy of foreclosures, repossessions, personal bankruptcies, and increased unemployment.

My legal, economic, and business background, as well as my years of experience in senior corporate positions in banking, consumer product, and market information services, could have led me to focus more extensively on the aforementioned conditions. It could have led me to provide ample, accurate, and statistical information to support the above contentions. However, the purpose of this book is not to present one more economic and financial dissertation in addition to the controversial ones already publicly available. My objective is to outline those conditions solely as an introduction, as a frame of reference, for the assessment and evaluation of the real causes of the present crisis, which are of a *spiritual nature*. It is essential to do so under the guidance of the Holy Spirit and based on precise biblical texts, *"for our struggle is not against flesh and blood, but against the rulers, against the powers, against the world forces of this darkness, against the spiritual forces of wickedness in the heavenly places"* (Eph. 6:12).

Thus, the fundamental purpose for writing this book is to generate spiritual awareness among Christians and non-Christians about what is actually happening and alert them according to the Scriptures about what is to come. That should allow them to verify for themselves what prophecies written thousands of years ago say about unfolding current events and should encourage them to diligently seek God's protection: *"Because you have kept the word of My perseverance, I also will keep you from the hour of testing, that hour which is about to come upon the whole world, to test those who dwell upon the earth. I am coming quickly; hold fast to what you have, in order that no one take your crown"* (Rev. 3:10–11). This is infinitely more important than to provide counsel as to how to safeguard one's worldly possessions or to attempt to gain an understanding of present events from a material point of view, which would be to no avail.

People are currently confused and bewildered by a situation that they do not fully comprehend and have lost confidence in their governments and their political, business, and even religious leaders—and with good reason.

Their distrust has particularly focused on governments, the banking and financial systems and institutions, as well as on large corporations. People feel that leadership in general has betrayed their confidence, while showing a lack of responsibility and disregard for sound management practices, transparency, and moral and ethical principles, let alone spiritual ones.

The Word of God, which by His grace I have taught for the last thirty-five years as a lay teacher, refers to the present time as the latter days, as the period that precedes the rescue of the true church from the Great Tribulation, the Antichrist, the false prophet, and the war of Armageddon, which will take place prior to the return of the Lord Jesus Christ to Earth. The Word of God tells us about the signs that will appear in the latter days, most importantly:

- *Wars and rumors of wars:* The prophecies say that *"you will be hearing of wars and rumors of wars. See that you are not frightened, for those things must take place, but that is not yet the end"* (Matt. 24:6). This scripture offers a warning from Jesus Christ to His disciples, but it is actually also addressed to us today and to all those who heed His word. His counsel reassures us not to fear, for fear is the enemy of our faith. Our banner should be: *"The Lord is for me; I will not fear. What can man do to me?"* (Ps. 118:6).

- *Religious conflicts* and intolerance are also afflicting many areas of the world, and minority segments of the population continue to be discriminated against and exposed to violence. In a number of countries where persecution is ostensible and gaining momentum, Christians are among those discriminated against, as addressed in the Scriptures.

- *Natural disasters* in various places, such as earthquakes and hurricanes, famine and pestilence, have increased in frequency and intensity, as predicted by the Lord Jesus Christ Himself when describing it as *"birth pangs"* (Matt. 24:7–8) as the time of His coming approaches.

Through the following pages you will be able to ascertain the accuracy of Bible prophesies about the latter days (our time). The vast majority of these prophecies have been fulfilled already, and for the remainder the stage is set for them to occur. Mathematically, the statistical probability of a coincidence relative to so many prophesies occurring as predicted would be in the billionth power, which is tantamount to impossible. For those that ask for a sign from God to believe, this is a most clear and definite one. I have divided this discussion of end-time prophecies into five parts, which make up the following five chapters: "Warnings," "Spiritual Signs," "External Signs," "The Events to Follow," and "Conclusions and Admonishments."

I believe that the Word of God is *"living and active and sharper than any two-edged sword, and piercing as far as the division of soul and spirit, of both joints and marrow, and able to judge the thoughts and intentions of the heart"* (Heb. 4:12). Thus, I view the role and responsibility of a Christian worker or writer to be in accordance with 2 Timothy 2:15: *"Be diligent to present yourself approved to God as a workman who does not need to be ashamed, accurately handling the word of truth."* This scripture has always guided me in hundreds of Bible classes over the last three decades, and now in this writing. I believe that in teaching or writing, the preeminence corresponds to the Word of God, and one's role should be only to add comments to help in its interpretation, to harmonize it around the theme provided by the Lord, and to highlight how it is applicable to the times we live in and, most certainly, to ourselves.

In reading the Scriptures, however, we should be reminded that words and punctuation marks are only symbols, and that the revelation and spiritual meaning of a message can only be provided by the Holy Spirit under prayer and through spiritual discernment: *"Not that we are adequate in ourselves to consider anything as coming from ourselves, but our adequacy is from God, who also made us adequate as servants of a new covenant, not of the letter but of the Spirit; for the letter kills, but the Spirit gives life"* (2 Cor. 3:5–6).

This is all the more important because, as warned in the Scriptures, *"false Christs and false prophets will arise and will show great signs and wonders, so as to mislead, if possible, even the elect"* (Matt. 24:24). This is the *"spirit of the antichrist, of which you have heard…is coming, and now…is already in the world"* (1 John 4:3). Indeed, they are already in our midst in worldly organizations, in religious sects, on television, and in videos and publications, distorting the Word of God with astute and deceptive interpretations and assuming an authority that they do not have. This is why you yourself must gain knowledge of the Word of God under the guidance of the Holy Spirit.

Chapter 2

WARNINGS

The Revelation of Jesus Christ, which God gave Him to His bond servants, the things that must shortly take place; and He sent and communicated it by His angel to His bond servant John, who bore witness to the word of God and to the testimony of Jesus Christ, even to all that he saw. Blessed is he who reads and those who hear the words of this prophecy, and heed the things which are written in it; for the time is near.
—Revelation 1:1–3

What Is a Warning?

Without becoming too dogmatic, a *warning*:

1. Is sign or a notice of precaution or advice, or an intimation, orally or in writing, about future events or conditions that could have a negative impact or influence on the party or person to whom it is addressed;

2. Usually involves a description of those future events or conditions posing a threat to the warned party or person;

3. Might include, explicitly or implicitly, a word of advice as to how to deal or face up to alerted or forewarned conditions or events, thereby involving counsel or a word of caution relative to the actual warning.

Mankind is reluctant to warnings, however, as they are naturally rebellious and often adverse to reading, hearing, or abiding by any message that, in their perception, constrains their "freedom" or their "right" to choose their own course—even if such warnings come from God or are established by tradition, as the often-quoted principle that states, "Your right ends where the right of others begins." Warning signs are everywhere: No Trespassing, No Smoking, No Parking, Stop, Speed Limit, Dangerous Curb, No Littering, Slow: Children Present, and so on. So are legal, fiscal, municipal warnings, and plain codes regarding social conduct and community rules of behavior. Worldly men need only receive such a warning for it to trigger in them some sort of reaction to challenge it. The Word says that this is so because *"the heart is more deceitful than all else And is desperately sick; Who can understand it?"* (Jer. 17:9). Proverbs 17:19 adds, *"He who loves transgression loves strife"*.

Regrettably, this attitude toward worldly warnings and intimations is also present before the Word of God. Jesus Christ often had to repeat, *"Verily, verily I say unto you,"* and *"Hear, those who have ears to hear,"* in order to draw attention, for He was intimately aware of the nature of men. They are quick to speak but slow to hear, and even then they filter words through their own "wisdom," through their worldly culture, knowledge, and intelligence, which most often limits their understanding; for wisdom comes from God, who offers it freely to whoever request it with faith (James 1:5).

God is Spirit, and His Word can only be discerned through His Spirit. For:

> *Now we have received, not the spirit of the world, but the Spirit Who is from God, that we might know the things freely given to us by God, which things we also speak, not in words taught by human wisdom,*

but in those taught by the Spirit, combining spiritual thoughts with spiritual words. But the natural man does not accept the things of the Spirit of God, for they are foolishness to him, and he cannot understand them, because they are spiritually appraised.
—1 CORINTHIANS 2:12–14

SPIRITUAL WARNINGS

It requires faith to hear and meditate on the warnings set forth in the Word of God. These messages are also full of grace and compassion, in that at the same time it cautions about the things to come in the latter days, it also provides hope, reassurance, and a way out. The option is always ours, for the free will that God has given men is a prerequisite for true love and communion with Him, which is all that God requires from us.

The question is not whether we feel or acknowledge that the warnings received are right, or whether these are in line with our logic and expectations. It takes only common sense to know that our intelligence and knowledge are indeed finite and insignificant *vis-à-vis* the wisdom of God. While the Lord reassures us of His constant desire to pardon us from our sins and inequities, at the same time He has told us through the prophet Isaiah: *"'For My thoughts are not your thoughts, neither are your ways My ways,' declares the Lord. For as the heavens are higher than the earth, so are My ways higher than your ways, and My thoughts than your thoughts"* (Isa. 55:8–9).

The Lord further reassures us through Isaiah 55:11 that *"so will My word be which goes forth from My mouth; It will not return to Me empty, Without accomplishing what I desire, And without succeeding in the matter for which I sent it."* No matter what it may seem to us, faith means to place our trust in God, to have confidence in what He has told us or warned us about. Regrettably, we are in the midst of a spiritual battle that greatly exceeds our capabilities and understanding, and we will never make it without His guidance and protection. Jesus Christ warned us, *"I am the vine, you are the branches; he that abides in Me, and I in him, he bears much fruit; for apart from Me you can do nothing"* (John 15:5).

How appropriate and timely that warning is, because men have become proud and arrogant, blind to see and deaf to hear the word of the Lord, and they have placed themselves outside His will. The Scriptures are abundantly clear about how men would be in the latter days, which is the time we are now living in:

> *But realize this, that in the last days difficult times will come. For men will be lovers of self, lovers of money, boastful, arrogant, revilers, disobedient to parents, ungrateful, unholy, unloving, irreconcilable, malicious gossips, without self-control, brutal, haters of good, treacherous, reckless, conceited, lovers of pleasure rather than lovers of God; holding the form of godliness, although they have denied its power; Avoid such men as these.*
> —2 Timothy 3:1–5

What a forthright and accurate description of what is going on, *"for as [a man] thinks within himself, so he is"* (Prov. 23:7). This clarifies the warning to "avoid such men as these" (2 Tim. 3:5), since as they think, so will they act.

But how can we separate ourselves from evil men? They seem to be everywhere, to increasingly control most everything, to hold worldly power, and to use it for their own selfish purposes. The Lord has warned us: *"Do not be envious of evil men, Nor desire to be with them; For their minds devise violence, And their lips talk of trouble"* (Prov. 24:1–2). And He reaffirms in Psalm 37:1–5:

> *Fret not yourself because of evildoers, Be not envious toward wrongdoers. For they will wither quickly like the grass, And fade like the green herb. Trust in the Lord, and do good; Dwell in the land and cultivate faithfulness. Delight yourself in the Lord; And He will give you the desires of your heart. Commit your way to the Lord, Trust also in Him, and He will do it.*

Keep in mind these words as we scrutinize the prophetic scriptures that follow, and have no fear for the Lord is with you, or you would not be reading His message.

We are further warned:

> *Know this first of all, that in the last days mockers will come with their mocking, following after their own lust, and saying, "Where is the promise of His coming? For ever since the fathers fell asleep, all continues just as it was from the beginning of creation." For them that maintain this, it escapes their notice that by the word of God the heavens existed long ago and the earth was formed out of water and by water, through which the world at that time was destroyed being flooded with water. But the present heavens and earth by His word are being reserved for fire, kept for the day of judgment and destruction of ungodly men.*
>
> —2 Peter 3:3–7

Worldly men fail to understand the immensity of God's love and His patience and desire for none to perish in the expectation that they may repent from their evil ways. For how long is eternity? If we were to meditate carefully on this concept alone, ungodly men would realize just what is at stake and how little the Lord requires from us to join Him in His kingdom: *"But to do justice, to love kindness, And to walk humbly with your God"* (Mic. 6:8).

Psalm 19:1 says that *"the heavens are telling of the glory of God; And their expanse is declaring the works of His hands."* One would need to be blind not to see it or very unwise to believe that it all came into being by some colossal and casual cosmic harmonization. Therefore, there is no excuse for those that believe that way, as revealed in Romans 1:20: *"For since the creation of the world His invisible attributes , His eternal power and divine nature, have been clearly seen, being understood through what has been made, so that they are without excuse."*

This book is meant to speak to the heart of those that the Lord will lead to read it. The sincere desire of my heart is that they may be many, for their sake, because *"the Spirit explicitly says that in the later times some will fall away from the faith, paying attention to deceitful spirits and doctrines of demons"* (1 Tim. 4:1). How are we to combat the forces of evil, spiritual deception, the seduction of money, the temptations of the flesh, and the fear of the unknown? The Lord says:

> *Therefore, take up the full armor of God, that you may be able to resist in the evil day, and having done everything, to stand firm. Stand firm therefore, having girded your loins with the truth, and having put on the breastplate of righteousness, and having shod your feet with the preparation of the gospel of peace; in addition to all, taking up the shield of faith with which you will be able to extinguish all the flaming missiles of the evil one. And take the helmet*

of salvation, and the sword of the Spirit, which is the word of God.

—Ephesians 6:13–17

Notice that the armor of God is for defense (truth, righteousness, the gospel of peace, the shield of faith, and the helmet of salvation), which means that *"if God is for us, who is against us?"* (Rom. 8:31). Conversely, the Word of God is also the sword of the Spirit, the most powerful weapon for spiritual warfare, as it is the representation of Jesus Christ Himself (John 1:1), who upholds all things by the word of His power (Heb. 1:3) and is capable of destroying all fortresses of evil and all sinful works. In these latter days, let us be close to Christ, for He said, *"I am the way, and the truth, and life; no one goes to the Father but through Me"* (John 14:6).

———

Dear reader, consider that a warning from the Lord is a blessing that, if heeded, can change your life and lead you to the way of God's eternal kingdom. Do not rely on what the world is doing, *"for the gate is wide, and the way is broad that leads to destruction, and there are many who enter through. For the gate is small and the way is narrow that leads to life, and there are few who find it"* (Matt. 7:13–14).

The Word further warns us about when the Antichrist manifests itself: *"There was given to him a mouth speaking arrogant words and blasphemies, and authority to act for forty-two months was given to him"* (Rev. 13:5). This is the first half of the seven-year period of the Great Tribulation announced by biblical prophecy and Jesus Christ Himself (Matt. 24:9); it is to come immediately after the latter days we are presently living in. As noted above, this will be the period announced in Revelation 3:10, the *"hour of testing, that hour which is about to come upon the whole world,"* but from which hour the Lord has promised to safeguard all who have kept His Word. This promise now extends to all who become true believers, and the time to ensure His protection is now.

Chapter 3
SPIRITUAL SIGNS

What Is a Spiritual Sign?

The word *sign*, which originates from the Latin word *signum*, has a diversity of meanings, from "designating an object" or "a mark, an image or a seal." Fundamentally, though, it applies to an indication perceived by the senses or by reason. The Webster Dictionary of the American Language also recognizes a sign as "an act or happening regarded as a miraculous demonstration of divine will or power."[1] In this chapter we will be guided by this later definition but will significantly expand on it based on the Word of God.

In the latter days there will also be signs that do not originate from God but from the forces of evil, which will confuse many (Rev. 16:14; 19:20). These demonic signs will ostensibly appear as of a religious nature and will be backed up by fake miracles and wonders displayed by false Christs and prophets who will lead many astray (Mark 13:22). We will address in this book the signs given to us through Bible prophecy for the latter days so as to eradicate any doubts about what we should expect and in order to be prepared to clearly discern those signs from the deception that will be orchestrated by the enemy of our souls.

The Greatest Spiritual Sign

The greatest sign ever given to men was the appearance of Jesus Christ on Earth, His life, His words and deeds, and finally His death at the cross, through which men's salvation became possible: *"For God so loved the world, that He gave His only begotten Son, that whoever believes in Him should not perish, but have eternal life"* (John 3:16). His coming was necessary because men misused the free will granted to them and disregarded the grace to be guided by God's Word and His Spirit. That is why the essence of sin is rebellion against God's will. The Word reveals that God's dispensation in providing the way to salvation through Jesus Christ became the only alternative for men, who had unrepentantly fallen into sin: *"There is none righteous, not even one; There is none who understands, There is none who seeks for God; All have turned aside, together they have become useless; There is none who does good, There is not even one"* (Rom. 3:10–12; see also Ps. 14:1–3; 53:1–4).

The first coming of Jesus Christ was foretold in the Old Testament by thirty seven different and explicit prophesies, all fulfilled as corroborated in the New Testament.

1. He was born of a woman (Gen. 3:15, fulfilled in Gal. 4:4).

2. He was a descendant of Abraham (Gen. 12:3, fulfilled in Matt. 1:1).

3. He was a descendant of Isaac (Gen. 17:19, fulfilled in Luke 3:34).

4. He was a descendant of Jacob (Num. 24:17, fulfilled in Matt. 1:2).

5. He was from the tribe of Judah (Gen. 49:10, fulfilled in Luke 3:33).

6. He was heir to the throne of David (Isa. 9:7, fulfilled in Luke 1:32–33).

7. He was born in Bethlehem (Mic. 5:2, fulfilled in Luke 2:4–7).

8. He was born at the appointed time (Dan. 9:25, fulfilled in Luke 2:1–2).

9. He was born of a virgin (Isa. 7:14, fulfilled in Luke 1:26–31).

10. He escaped the slaughter of the innocent (Jer. 31:15, fulfilled in Matt. 10. 2:16–18).

11. He was called out of Egypt (Hos. 11:1, fulfilled in Matt. 2:14–15).

12. He was preceded by a forerunner ((Mal. 3:1, fulfilled in Luke 7:24,27).

13. He was declared the Son of God (Ps. 2:7, fulfilled in Matt. 3:17).

14. His ministry would be in Galilee (Isa. 9:1–2, fulfilled in Matt. 4:13–16).

15. He would be a prophet (Deut. 18:15, fulfilled in Acts 3:20, 22).

16. He was sent to heal the brokenhearted (Isa. 61:1–2, fulfilled in Luke 4:18–19).

17. He was rejected by His people, the Jews (Isa. 53:3, fulfilled in John 1:11; Luke 23:18).

Spiritual Signs

18. He was a priest after the order of Melchizedek (Ps. 110:4, fulfilled in Heb. 5:5–6).

19. He had a triumphal entry into Jerusalem (Zech. 9:9, fulfilled in Mark 11:7–11).

20. He was betrayed by a friend (Ps. 41:9, fulfilled in Luke 22:47–48).

21. He was sold for thirty pieces of silver (Zech. 11:12, fulfilled in Matt. 26:15).

22. He was accused by false witnesses (Ps. 35:11, fulfilled in Mark 14:57–58).

23. He was silent before His accusers (Isa. 53:7, fulfilled in Mark 15:4–5).

24. He was spat upon and smitten (Isa. 50:6, fulfilled in Matt. 26:67).

25. He was hated without reason (Ps. 35:19, fulfilled in John 15:24–25).

26. He died for the ungodly (Isa. 53:5, fulfilled in Rom. 5:6–8).

27. He was crucified with transgressors (Isa. 53:12, fulfilled in Mark 15:27–28).

28. He was pierced through hands and feet (Zech. 12:10, fulfilled in John 20:27).

29. He was scorned and mocked (Ps. 22:7–8, fulfilled in Luke 23:35).

30. He was given vinegar and gall (Ps. 69:21, fulfilled in Matt. 27:34).

31. Nonetheless, He prayed for his enemies (Ps. 109:4, fulfilled in Luke 23:34).

32. Soldiers gambled for His coat (Ps. 22:17–18, fulfilled in Matt. 27:35–36).

33. His bones were not broken (Ps. 34:20, fulfilled in John 19:32–36).

34. His side was pierced (Zech. 12:10, fulfilled in John 19:34).

35. He was buried with the rich (Isa. 53:9, fulfilled in Matt. 27:57–60).

36. He rose from the dead (Ps. 16:10, fulfilled in Mark 16:6–7).

37. He ascended to God's right hand (Ps. 68:18, fulfilled in Mark 16:19; 1 Cor. 15:4; Eph. 4:8).

The reason for explicitly listing the most impressive assembly of fulfilled prophesies above is for the reader to acknowledge on his own that this evidence represents an unequivocal *sign from God*.[2] The probability of a coincidence—a nonexistent term in the field of statistics—is virtually none. These scriptures cover a time expanse of thousands of years and their transcription has been safeguarded by scribes, prophets, apostles, and recognized men of God of various backgrounds living in different times under diverse circumstances and confronting difficult challenges. Yet, the accuracy and concordance of their writings and prophesies are flawless. I encourage you to read them under prayer, and the Lord will uplift your heart and give you a deeper understanding of Jesus Christ, God's Word, and what lies ahead. It does not make any difference whether you are already a Christian, an agnostic, or an atheist; the Word of God is powerful to knock down fortresses and dispel unbelief. Do not allow pride to interfere, for, *"If any one supposes that he knows anything, he has not yet known as he ought to know"* (1 Cor. 8:2).

It is essential to understand that *"in the beginning was the Word, and the Word was with God, and the Word was God"* (John 1:1). Thus, pseudo-religious people and even Bible interpreters should not make a cult of the "letter" (2 Cor. 3:6: *"for the letter kills"*). Instead, as noted earlier in this writing, they should seek the revelation of the Word through the Holy Spirit. Jesus Christ confronted the religious Jews of His days on earth (the scribes and the Pharisees) when He told them, *"You search the Scriptures because you think that in them you have eternal life; it is these that testify about Me"* (John 5:39). Thus, our objective must be to have a *personal and loving relationship with Christ* with the help of the Holy Spirit and built upon the foundation of His Word, to the glory of the Father. If we can do that, "loving our neighbor" and good works will simply flow from that relationship, and we will surely come into God's grace. Lord, let it be so.

Hatred and Evil

The increased manifestation of all forms of evil is another powerful sign of the latter days. People have difficulty in understanding the relentless hatred of our spiritual enemy toward us; that enemy abhors serving men as required by God, as they despise what in their eyes is greatly below their past glory and dignity.

The pride of our enemy was tested, and inequity was found in Lucifer and one third of the angels of heaven that followed him.

> *How you have fallen from heaven, O star of the morning, son of the dawn! You have been cut down to the earth, You who have weakened the nations! But you said in your heart, "I will ascend to heaven; I will raise my throne above the stars of God, And I will sit on the mount of assembly In the recesses of the north. I will ascend above the heights of the clouds; I will make myself like the Most High." Nevertheless, you will be thrust down to Sheol, To the recesses of the pit.*
>
> —Isaiah 14:12–15

While rebellion is not an unusual situation on Earth, as it stems from the very nature of men, it represented an unpardonable sin for a cherubim (Lucifer), an angelic being who lived before the very throne of God.

His rebellion was countered by the archangel Michael, along with two thirds of the angels, those who remained faithful to the Lord.

> *And there was war in heaven, Michael and his angels waging war with the dragon. The dragon and his angels waged war, and they were not strong enough, and there was no longer a place found for them in heaven. And the great dragon was thrown down, the serpent of old who is called the devil and Satan, who deceives the whole world; he was thrown down to the earth, and his angels were thrown down with him. Then I heard a loud voice in heaven, saying, "Now the salvation, and the power, and the kingdom of our God and the authority of His Christ have come, for the accuser of our brethren has been thrown down, he who accuses them before our God day and night. And they overcame him because of the blood of the Lamb and because of the word of their testimony,*

and they did not love their life even when faced with death. For this reason, rejoice, O heavens and you who dwell in them. Woe to the earth and the sea, because the devil has come down to you, having great wrath, knowing that he has only a short time."
—Revelation 12:7–12

The most essential conclusions from the above scriptures are:

- The battle between good and evil, while we are in the midst of it, greatly exceeds our understanding, our own strengths and capabilities, and the perimeters of our lives and surroundings. It started in heaven, as Lucifer pretended to be like God, and one-third of the angels followed him, a desecration defeated by God through the archangel Michael and the faithful angels under him.

- Satan and the fallen angels were cast out of heaven and thrown down to Earth. Under those circumstances, men, God's creation, would have been lost, because Satan's first deception involved Adam and Eve, and through them, sin entered into the world. That sin would have prevailed in it, separating us from God, if not because of Christ Jesus.

- Thus, salvation became possible only through the vicarious offering of God's only begotten Son, the Lord Jesus Christ, who sealed Satan and his fallen angels' defeat and condemnation at the cross.

- While Jesus Christ paid the debt of sin for all mankind, redemption is only possible for them that believe in Him, for those who place their trust in Him and live by His word. That supreme act of love was a manifestation of the very nature of God: *"For God is love"* (1 John 4:8).

- The infinite nature of His sacrifice cannot be grasped through our intellect but through the witness of the Holy Spirit to our spirit (Rom. 8:16). For while Jesus Christ *"existed in the form of God, did not regard equality with God a thing to be grasped, but emptied Himself, taking form of a bond-servant, and being made in the likeness of men. Being found in appearance as a man, He humbled Himself by becoming obedient to the point of death, even death on a cross. Therefore, also God highly exalted Him, and bestowed on Him the name that is above every name, so that at the name of Jesus every knee will bow, of those who are in heaven and on earth and under the earth, and that every tongue confess that Jesus Christ is the Lord, to the glory of God the Father"* (Phil. 2:6–11).

- Understanding and accepting the above truth provides a solid foundation for our salvation and the fulfillment of our call, but it also reveals the horrendous consequences for those who reject Christ Jesus. There is no possible compromise on this, no middle ground: *"He who believes in Him is not judged; he who does not believe has been judged already, because he has not believed in the name of the only begotten Son of God"* (John 3:18).

- The above scriptures also explain the wrath of the enemy in these later days and the upsurge of evil in all its forms. Satan knows that he is condemned and that his time is running out, and his vengeance against God is to take with him as many souls as he can.

Jesus Christ, however, has reassured His followers: *"Behold, I have given you authority to tread upon serpents and scorpions, and over all the power of the enemy, and nothing will injure you"* (Luke 10:18–19). But be very clear on this: our sufficiency is in Him only. There are no intercessors or intermediaries, for without Him we cannot do anything other than be exposed to the wrath and power of the enemy.

SPIRITUAL SIGNS OF JESUS' COMING

Matthew 24 conveys the Lord's response to the questions from His disciples about the signs preceding His return to Earth.

> *As He was sitting on the Mount of Olives, the disciples came to Him privately, saying, "Tell us, when will these things happen, and what will be the*

sign of Your coming, and of the end of the age?" And Jesus answered and said to them, "See to it that no one misleads you. For many will come in My name, saying, 'I am the Christ,' and will mislead many. You will be hearing of wars and rumors of wars. See that you are not frightened, for those things must take place, but that is not yet the end. For nation will rise against nation, and kingdom against kingdom, and in various places there will be famines and earthquakes.... Then they will deliver you to tribulation, and will kill you, and you will be hated by all nations because of My name. At that time many will fall away and will betray one another and hate one another.... Because lawlessness is increased, most people's love will grow cold. But the one who endures to the end, he will be saved. This gospel of the kingdom shall be preached in the whole world as a testimony to all the nations, and then the end will come.

—MATTHEW 24:3–7, 9–10, 12–14

Matthew 24:4–5

"See to it that no one misleads you. For many will come in My name, saying, 'I am the Christ,' and will mislead many."

We have seen already many impersonators of Christ throughout history, and many more that without using His name have pretended to act in a messianic way. A sign of the latter days is that these misrepresentations will increase around the world. Their main purpose is not only to confuse and mislead but to deviate the attention of men from Jesus Christ.

Spiritual Signs

> *By this you know the Spirit of God: every spirit that confesses that Jesus Christ has come in the flesh is from God; and every spirit that does not confess Jesus is not from God; this is the spirit of the antichrist, of which you have heard that is coming, and now it is already in the world.*
>
> —1 JOHN 4:2–3

Notice that there is a difference between the "spirit of the antichrist," which has been in our midst ever since Jesus Christ appeared on Earth, and the *person* of the Antichrist, a man who is to be possessed by Satan, who will make his appearance *after* the latter days and during the first forty-two months (three and a half years) of the Great Tribulation period (Matt. 24:21). The Word refers to the Antichrist as *"the man of lawlessness... the son of destruction, who opposes and exalts himself above every so-called god or object of worship, so that he takes his seat in the temple of God, displaying himself as being God.... whom the Lord will slay with the breath of His mouth and bring to an end by the appearance of His coming"* (2 Thess. 2:3–4, 8).

As previously noted in this book, I will be first addressing herein that which pertains to the latter days. However, in the fifth chapter, a brief reference will be made to the Rapture of the church, the Great Tribulation period that is to follow, the triumphal second coming of the Lord Jesus Christ, His millennial kingdom on Earth and the merger of it into the eternal kingdom of God, the Great White Throne Judgment, the creation of a new Heaven and a new Earth, and the final journey into eternity. This chronology, thoroughly supported by scriptures and concordances, interwoven with the author's commentaries, will hopefully facilitate the readers' understanding of what is to come.

Matthew 24:6

> *You will be hearing of wars and rumors of wars. See that you are not frightened, for those things must take place, but that is not yet the end.*

When you tell people about this sign, they often respond that all through history there have been wars and rumors of wars. However, never until these latter days have men possessed weapons of mass destruction capable of rapidly extinguishing life on Earth.

Never before has the threat of war represented a warning to all nations either directly or indirectly involved in a conflict. The world has become a "common space," and men instigated by Satan and his followers exploit the threat of international, regional, and national conflicts in pursuit of their veiled objective to bring such disorder into the world so as to justify the creation of a new order and of a world government, along with a leader under Satan to rule it: the Antichrist. Those conditions will be partly attained by the enemy because God will grant to him authority to do that during a period of three and a half years, as previously noted, as a test for men. This period will be one *"as has not occurred since the beginning of the world until now, nor ever will"* (Matt. 24:21), when the appearance of the Antichrist will take place *"in accord with the activity of Satan, with all power and signs and false wonders"* (2 Thess. 2:9). All this will finally lead up to the Battle of Armageddon, the final judgment of the Antichrist and the false prophet upon the glorious return of the Lord Jesus Christ to Earth, and ultimately to Satan's condemnation at the end of the millennium kingdom of Christ on Earth, as we will address in the following chapters.

Matthew 24:7

> *For nation will rise against nation, and kingdom against kingdom, and in various places there will be famines and earthquakes.*

Again, there are few isolated, local conflicts around the world in these days because the major world powers have forced the nations to align themselves either ideologically, religiously, financially, militarily, geographically, in trade groups, or in the exploitation of key resources. Whereas in appearance nations and kingdoms are depicted as being in separate conflicts with each other, the backing and support from the major nations actually expands those confrontations into regional and continental wars. This is why, while the world has the capacity to feed all nations, the curse of famine remains in a number of regions as a consequence of the rivalry amongst existing power blocks.

As for earthquakes and other natural disasters, it is a scientifically recorded fact that in recent years such phenomena has increased in frequency and intensity, as prophesied by Jesus Christ Himself. More and more we are exposed to unprecedented natural events in terms of their power and capacity to cause damage and destruction.

The world is demanding recognition by its leaders of the magnitude of unfolding climatic changes and their consequences, and on the need for them to agree on new policies to contain increasing calamities. While the intentions of some are good, the solutions are out of their reach. The best thing that the world could do is to pray about it and seek God's guidance and protection, but men are focused in their own selfish interests and limited ability to deal with the problem, to no avail. It is like King Nimrod's attempt to reach the throne of God by building the Tower of Babel: an impossible and useless exercise.

Matthew 24:9

> *Then they will deliver you to tribulation, and will kill you, and you will be hated by all nations because of My name.*

Whereas the above sign pertains to the Great Tribulation period itself, in these preceding latter days the Lord is warning us about those difficult times to come so we may now recognize and understand that presently, Christian persecution, in some places, has only begun. Persecution against Christians our days is not only the result of religious bigotry but is a consequence of our reaction to abominations such as abortion, the legalization of gay practices, sexual promiscuity, the prohibition of prayer in public schools, immorality in mass media, corruption in the public and private sectors, drug trafficking, and violence promoted by the free access to guns and deadly weaponry, just to name some of the most visible examples.

Awareness about the meaning of these spiritual signs is fundamental to prepare ourselves for the events that will ensue. We must be grounded in the Word and walk very close to the Lord, because deception will abound. The Lord has already warned us against false prophets and false Christs, who through the use of signs and wonders will mislead multitudes.

Imagine for a moment just how difficult it will be for Christians (and needless to say non-Christians) who are not fully conversant with the latter-day prophecies to understand why evil seems to progressively dominate the world. What you read in the newspapers, what you see on television, what you hear on the radio, what you experience in the streets all points out immorality, violence, disorder, selfishness, hatred, and what seems to be a prevalence of evil in most areas surrounding our lives. These events have caused some to question, Why is God not intervening? Why is He allowing this to happen? Why has He abandoned us?

The response is in the Word of God:

> *This I say, and affirm together with the Lord, that you walk no longer just as the Gentiles also walk, in the futility of their mind, being darkened in their understanding, excluded from the life of God because of the ignorance that is in them, because of the hardness of their heart.*
> —EPHESIANS 4:17–18

Further, the Lord has said:

> *Consider it all joy, my brethren, when you encounter various trials, knowing that the testing of your faith produces endurance. And let endurance have its perfect result, so that you be made perfect and complete, lacking in nothing. But if any of you lacks wisdom, let him ask of God, who gives to all men generously and without reproach, and it will be given to him. But let him ask in faith without any doubting, for the one who doubts is like the surf of the sea, driven and tossed by the wind.*
> —JAMES 1:2–6

Thus, let us be humble before the Lord: *"A wise man will hear and increase in learning, And a man of* understanding will acquire wise counsel.... The fear of the Lord is the beginning of knowledge; Fools despise wisdom and instruction" (Prov. 1:5, 7).

Let us become aware and take due notice that God has *"put all things in subjection under His feet* [Jesus Christ]...*He left nothing that is not subject to Him. But now we do not yet see all things subjected to Him"* (Heb. 2:8). This is the greatest test of our faith, of our confidence in Him—that although evil appears to be winning the battle in these latter days, it is only for a season and for a purpose, for *"the proof of your faith, being more precious than gold which is perishable, even though tested by fire, may be found to result in praise and glory and honor at the revelation of Jesus Christ"* (1 Pet. 1:7).

Matthew 24:10

> *At that time many will fall away and will betray one another and hate one another.*

If your house is built on sand, floods will wash it away. Our faith has to be built on the rock of our salvation (Matt. 7:24). And the prophetic word is clear: our faith will be tested by trials and by fire. The Lord has forewarned us that we must nourish our spiritual strength in these latter days, for *"you know who restrains him now, so that in his time he might be revealed. For the mystery of lawlessness is already at work; only He* [the Holy Spirit] *who now restrains will do so until He is taken out of the way. And then the lawless one will be revealed whom the Lord shall slay with the breath of His mouth and bring to an end by the appearance of His coming"* (2 Thess. 2:6–8).

Let us not be among those who fall away from the faith when the going gets rough, as Peter did when he jumped out of the boat to walk on water toward where the Lord was waiting for him. He was doing well, and he was the first one to offer Jesus to go toward Him in the middle of the storm; but the wind and the waves scared him and forced his eyes away from Christ, and he began to sink. Yet, the Lord stretched out His hand toward him, pulled Peter out of the water, and admonished him: *"You of little faith, why did you doubt?"* (Matt. 14:31).

So beware. Stormy spiritual days are ahead of us, with winds of adversity and waves of fear. But let us be close to Jesus, where we may stretch out our hand toward Him and receive His protection. Let us remain with our eyes fixed on Him so our faith may defeat fear and confusion and we may not stray from the Way.

Matthew 24:12

> *Because lawlessness is increased, most people's love will grow cold.*

In these latter days, spiritual deception is reaching unprecedented highs. Traditional justice and religious principles are giving way to legal systems, norms, and practices directly opposed to God's will. Legalized abortion, gay marriages, widespread corruption, deception, and violence are examples of the demonic contamination going on. Injustice is everywhere, and many people are discouraged.

Regarding people's love, the Lord is most compassionate when forewarning us that in the latter days *"love will grow cold."* It is currently evident that people have a distorted understanding of love, and that they do not comprehend its significance and importance. Please consider the following:

Agape: from the Greek *agapas*

Agape is love with a connotation of transcendence and respect, because it is the supreme and purest form of love. It is the love that God has for us, spiritual and unchanging, originating from His very nature, *"for God is love"* (1 John 4:8). It is the love that motivated the Father to offer Jesus Christ, His only begotten Son, as the reconciling offering for our sins, so that by trusting Him we may not perish but have eternal life (John 3:16). This is why the greatest and foremost commandment given to men is, *"You shall love the Lord your God with all your heart, and with all your soul, and with all your mind"* (Matt. 22:37). It must be love full of gratitude, for *"we love, because He first loved us"* (1 John 4:19) when we were lost and undeserving sinners. This is why *"by grace you have been saved through faith; and that not of yourself, it is the gift of God; not as a result of works, so that no one should boast"* (Eph. 2:8–9).

We must endeavor to comprehend God's love, to open our heart to Him, because He declares: *"Behold, I stand at the door and knock; if any one hears My voice and opens the door, I will come in to him and will dine with him, and he with Me"* (Rev. 3:20). The opening of the door of our heart points out to God's respect for our free will, while His "dining with us" depicts an act of traditional friendship and His desire for a personal relationship with us.

Friendship: from the Greek *filö*

Friendship relates more to love as a personal, intimate, and brotherly form of affection. Thus, the Lord further says that *"and a second* [commandment] *is like it, 'You shall love your neighbor as yourself'"* (Matt. 22:39). What an incommensurable blessing it is to sincerely recognize that Jesus is the best friend that one can possibly have, one that can be trusted above all your trials and difficulties and one who can keep you balanced when enjoying abundance and success (for either trials or successes will challenge your faith).

It is also most comforting to have Christian friends with whom one may congregate and share Christian values and experiences during our pilgrimage through life.

> *A man who has friends must be friendly, But there is a friend who sticks closer than a brother.*
> —PROVERBS 18:24, NKJV

It is a privilege and a blessing also to have friends amongst non-Christians, as a testimony to the unsaved, that you may win them over for the Lord through your loving conduct and understanding. The Lord encourages us to love everyone and to leave judgment to Him.

Eroticism: from the Greek *erōtikos*

Eroticism is a word descriptive of feelings and acts related to the flesh, to the preeminence of sexual excitement or behavior. Whereas there is nothing wrong with sexual relations within the boundaries of matrimony, uncontrolled eroticism frequently leads to erotomania (abnormally strong sexual desire) and promiscuity.

As commented in Chapter 4 in the section titled "The Surge of Emotionality vs. Spirituality," one of the signs of the latter days is the increasing subjection of the soul to the desires of the flesh, which the Word says represents enmity against God. This refers to the dominance of the carnal over the spiritual, which may even preclude men from discerning the things of the Spirit.

Eroticism in these later days is so widespread that people are losing track of the fact that the prevalence of the flesh over the soul also means the subjection of men's minds and emotions to the flesh, a dangerous way to perdition. Sinful Sodom and Gomorrah were destroyed by the Lord as an example for generations to come because of their widespread wickedness in general and eroticism and sexual perversion in particular: *"He condemned the cities of Sodom and Gomorrah to destruction by reducing them to ashes, having made them an example to those who would live ungodly lives thereafter"* (2 Pet. 2:6).

Matthew 24:13

But the one who endures to the end, he will be saved.

Thus, what should we do? The Word says, as previously noted, that we must *"take up the full armor of God, so that you will be able to resist in the evil day, and having done everything, to stand firm"* (Eph. 6:13).

This is why, in these latter days, the Lord exhorts us to:

Preach the word; be ready in season and out of season; reprove, rebuke, exhort, with great patience and instruction. For the time will come when they will not endure sound doctrine; but wanting to have their ears tickled, they will accumulate for themselves teachers in accordance with their own desires; and will turn their ears from the truth and will turn aside to myths. But you, be sober in all things, endure hardship, do the work of an evangelist, fulfill your ministry.
—2 Timothy 4:2–5

Endurance is a quality that we need to develop through obedience, discipline and sustained faith. Whereas *"by grace you have been saved through faith"* (Eph. 2:8), endurance requires that our faith be put to work, because *"if it has no works, [it] is dead, being by itself"* (James 2:17). Please consider Jesus, *"the author and perfecter of our faith, who for the joy set before Him endured the cross, despising the shame, and has sat down at the right hand of the throne of God...so that you will not grow weary and lose heart"* (Heb. 12:2–3).

From my own experience, even if I believed that my prayers were consistent with His Word, I have always known that no matter how much I may have beseeched Him, God was not going to do for me what He had made me capable of doing by myself. As a perfect Father, He knows that spiritual or physical laziness would weaken my character and leave my patience untested.

> *It is for discipline that you endure; God deals with you as with sons; for what son is there whom his father does not discipline?*
> —HEBREWS 12:7

The apostle Paul, comparing our pilgrimage through Earth as a race, urged us to *"run in such a way that [you] may win"* (1 Cor. 9:24). No athlete wins without intense training, pain, and effort. Christians should be no less. He further encourages, *"We desire that each of you show the same diligence so as to realize the full assurance of hope until the end, that you may not be sluggish, but imitators of those who through faith and patience inherit the promises"* (Heb. 6:11–12).

For this reason *"we must pay closer attention to what we have heard, so that we do not drift away from it"* (Heb. 2:1). And the Spirit echoes, "Hear, those who have ears to hear!"

Matthew 24:14

> *This gospel of the kingdom shall be preached in the whole world as a testimony to all the nations, and then the end will come.*

While Satan has spread his evil influence through the world's mass media, so has God spread His Word through his saints. The Bible continues to be the book most sold in the history of mankind. Priests, pastors, evangelists, preachers, and teachers of the Word have lifted up their voices everywhere. Missionaries have left no place on Earth where the gospel message has not been proclaimed. The question is, How many have truly heard the message? Nevertheless, we know that the Lord has determined, *"My word which goes forth from My mouth; It will not return to Me empty"* (Isa. 55:11), and that assurance should be good enough to encourage us to proclaim His Word.

Blessed are they that take part in the spreading of the Word, for the Lord says that *"you will go out with joy And be lead forth with peace; The mountains and the hills will break forth into shouts of joy before you, And the trees of the field will clap their hands"* (Isa. 55:12). What a glorious promise!

Chapter 4

EXTERNAL SIGNS

BY "EXTERNAL SIGNS of the latter days" we mean those events and conditions preannounced by prophecies that involve visible and tangible occurrences consistent with the Word of God.

We will divide them between prophecies already occurred and those preannounced for the later days, regarding which the Lord has said, *"Behold, I have told you in advance"* (Matt. 24:25).

SIGNS ALREADY OCCURRED

Return of the Jewish People to the Promised Land

This most important event was prophesied by several great men of God:

> *The Lord your God will restore you from captivity, and have compassion on you, and will gather you again from all the peoples where the Lord your God has scattered you. If your outcasts are at the end of the earth, from there the Lord your God will gather you, and from there He will bring you back.*
> —DEUTERONOMY 30:3–4

> *Therefore prophesy and say to them, "Thus says the Lord God, 'Behold, I will open your graves and cause you to come out of your graves, My people; and I*

will bring you into the land of Israel. Then you will know that I am the Lord, when I have opened your graves and cause you to come up out of your graves, My people. And I will put My Spirit within you, and you will come to life, and I will bring you on your own land.'"

—Ezekiel 37:12–14

Hear the word of the Lord, O nations, And declare in the coast lands afar off, And say: "He who scattered Israel will gather him And keep him as a shepherd keeps his flock." For the Lord has ransomed Jacob, and redeemed him from the hand of him who was stronger than he.

—Jeremiah 31:10–11

And He will lift up a standard for the nations And assemble the banished ones of Israel, And will gather the dispersed of Judah From the four corners of the earth.

—Isaiah 11:12

These prophecies were fulfilled through the United Nations Declaration of November 29, 1947, which enabled the establishment of the State of Israel upon the termination of the British Mandate over Palestine, which occurred on May 15, 1948.

Jewish people scattered all over the world began to return to the Promised Land, as prophesied, and a new nation was born.

Jerusalem Repossessed

In order to understand the spiritual significance of the repossession of Jerusalem by the Jewish people, which occurred in June of 1967 as Israel consolidated as a nation, one has to know the history of this city, which extends over approximately forty-five hundred years. Its name first appears in the Tablets of Ebra (c. 2400–2250 B.C.), and in the Scriptures it is recognized as "Salem" (Gen. 14:18). or "the City of Peace."

The first King of Jerusalem was Adoni-zedek, referred to in Joshua 10:1, and it was not mentioned again until David brought the head of Goliath there (1 Sam. 17:54). For this reason in his days it was also called "the City of David." After David's death, his son Solomon rebuilt the temple.

It was subsequently conquered by the Egyptians, the Assyrians, and the kings of Israel. Later, because of the abounding iniquities of the nation and after a siege of three years, it was taken over and completely destroyed by Nebuchadnezzar, king of Babylon; as a result the Jewish people were taken into captivity for seventy years in the year 586 B.C.

Subsequently, the city was restored, and the kingdom fell under Persian dominion. It was later placed under the Greek Empire until 167 B.C. At the time of Jesus Christ it was under the rule of Herod and members of his family, which actually were subservient to the Roman Empire, and the city was again destroyed in A.D. 70. Later, the Jews again rebuilt parts of the city through A.D. 135, but after a revolt against the Romans the city was once more destroyed, including the temple built by Solomon.

The Mohammedans, who called Jerusalem "the Holy" (*el-Khuds*), also occupied the city for a season, while in A.D. 326 it fell under the dominion of Constantine. Between A.D. 614 and 637 it was taken over from the Romans by the Persians, who lost it to the Arabs. They kept it until

A.D. 960. Later, the caliphs of Egypt placed it under their dominion, only to lose it to the Turcomans in A.D. 1073.

In 1099, during the First Crusade, Godfrey de Bouillon took the city from the Muslims, and de Bouillon became the first Christian king of Jerusalem. However, in 1187 the Sultan Saladin wrested the city from the Christians, and it remained for the most part in Muslim hands until the twentieth century.

No other city in the history of humanity has been exposed to so many battles, takeovers, destruction, and successive rebuilding efforts under so many different regimes and religions as Jerusalem, "the City of Peace." No other city has been, and still is, considered as a holy city by so many religions.[3]

This brief history of Jerusalem is meant to provide a frame of reference for the Bible prophesies dealing with the repossession of this city by the Jewish people in the later days, as follows:

> [Addressed to David] *Your house and your kingdom shall endure before Me forever; your throne shall be established forever.*
> —2 SAMUEL 7:16

> [Addressed to Solomon] *The Lord said to him: "I have heard your prayer and your supplication, which you have made before Me; I have consecrated this house which you have built by putting My name there forever, and My eyes and My heart will be there perpetually.*
> —1 KINGS 9:3

> *It will come about in that day that I will make Jerusalem a heavy stone for all the peoples; all who*

lift it will be severally injured. And all the nations of the earth will be gathered against it.
—Zechariah 12:3

And they will fall by the edge of the sword, and will be led captive into all the nations; and Jerusalem will be trampled under foot by the Gentiles until the times of the Gentiles are fulfilled.
—Luke 21:24

It is abundantly clear that the above prophesies have been fulfilled:

- Jerusalem has been under the sword for centuries, and indeed it became a "heavy stone for all the peoples" who died attacking it or defending it.

- The Jewish people were taken captive to Babylon for seventy years and were subsequently dispersed all over the world.

- The Gentiles did trample over Jerusalem for centuries, but their time has now been fulfilled.

- Jerusalem is today the capital of Israel against all odds, and while it is still surrounded by over 100 million Arabs and Muslims, the Lord has said that Israel will not be removed from there: *"'Also I will restore the captivity of my people Israel, And they will rebuild the ruined cities and live in them; They will also plant vineyards and drink their wine, And make gardens and eat their fruit. I will also plant them in their land, And they will not again be rooted out from their land which I have given them', Says the Lord your God"* (Amos 9:14–15). The first part of this prophecy has been fulfilled. As for the second one, regarding the non-removal of Israel from the Promised Land, as per the Lord's assurance it most definitely will not occur, as time will prove it.

The Flourishing of Israel

The extraordinary development of the State of Israel since its inception in May 1948 is in itself a miracle.

- Israel is small nation in a territory the size of New Jersey (20,330 sq. km), with a population of only 7.6 million. Of that number, 76.2 percent are Jews of various origins: Ashkenazim (of European background); Sephardim (from Spain, Portugal, southern Europe and North Africa); Oriental Jews (mainly from Islamic areas).

- Israel includes various religions: Judaism, Islam, Christianity, and Druze. It has two official languages, Hebrew and Arab, in addition to other languages spoken, principally English.

- Despite the above limitations and complexities, Israel has presently attained a gross domestic product of $195 billion and a per capita income of $26,178, which is in line with the most advanced nations of the world.

- It exports in excess of $50 billion worth of industrial products, minerals, and agricultural products per year, a powerful contribution to its balance of payment.

- Its literacy level is 96.9 percent, and it has been the source of a remarkable number of Nobel Prize winners in many fields, prominently science.

Israel has attained all of the above while at constant wars with its Arab neighbors since 1948 and until the present time.

The flourishing of Israel, recognized biblically as the "fig tree," has come to pass, as prophesied by the Lord Jesus in Matthew 24:32–33:

> *Now learn the parable from the fig tree: when its branch has already become tender and puts forth its leaves, you know that summer is near; even so, you too, when you see all these things, recognize that He is near, right at the door.*

Signs Occurring During the Later Days

Knowledge Will Increase

The Lord said to the prophet Daniel, *"Conceal these words and seal up the book until the end of time; many will go back and forth, and knowledge will increase"* (Dan. 12:4).

It is clear that the rapid development of means of

transportation, including its higher speed and lower costs, have made the world a smaller place. What seventy years ago took days and even weeks of traveling time, today can be accomplished in a matter of hours. Whereas the cultural and social implications from this development have been most positive, it has also brought about negative effects. Weapons and drug trafficking, the spread of contagious deceases, its application to warfare and regional conflicts—just to name a few—have been devastating. Daniel's prophecy was made twenty-two hundred years ago, and it has come to pass at these end times, as predicted.

Equally clear is that knowledge has increased, and, for that matter, exponentially. It is recognized in the scientific community that technology and applied sciences continue to advance at such a pace that those fields now double their knowledge base every year. Consumer and users' scientific applications are such that the old marketing admonition to develop products to "meet clients' needs and expectations" has become obsolete, for scientific innovation is way ahead of both, with new products and applications going far beyond clients and users' imagination. And so is the destructive power of new weapons of mass destruction, which align themselves with the Apostle Peter prophetic utterance: *"By His word the present heavens and earth are being reserved for fire, kept for the day of judgment and destruction of ungodly men"* (2 Pet. 3:7).

This external sign of the latter days manifests itself in such a variety of ways and forms that its biblical significance is neither grasped nor comprehended. Nonetheless, in these latter days, more than ever before, information and disinformation abound side by side, as the means of communication have expanded it into all fields of knowledge and life. As humanity moves forward into the age of deception, we must stay close to the truth, which is in Jesus Christ Himself. *"For the word of the cross is to those who are perishing foolishness, but to us who are being saved it is the power of God"* (1 Cor. 1:18).

The Lord says, *"The fear of the Lord is the beginning of knowledge; Fools despise wisdom and instruction"* (Prov. 1:7). He further admonishes, *"Acquire wisdom! Acquire understanding! Do not forget nor turn away from the words of my mouth"* (Prov. 4:5). But ungodly men turn on to their own understanding and pursue their own desires.

> *Thus says the Lord, "Let not a wise man boast of his wisdom, and let not the mighty man boast of his might, let not a rich man boast of his riches; but let him who boasts, boast of this, that he understands and knows Me, that I am the Lord who exercises loving kindness, justice and righteousness on earth; for I delight in these things," declares the Lord.*
> —JEREMIAH 9:23–24

Men who do not search for God but rather turn their eyes onto themselves, being selfish, egocentric, egotistical, and proud, remain aloof to the messages from God, blind to His testimonies and deaf to His Word. They pursue their own ways, because in their worldly wisdom that seems smart to them: *"There is a way which seems right to a man, But its end is the way of death"* (Prov. 14:12).

Warfare of the Mind

The enemy of our souls, also called the *"prince of the power of the air"* (Eph. 2:2), today controls mass media and takes advantage of current impressive technological advancement in the field of communication. Along with the increased technology and sophistication of the means of communication, significant efforts are being directed to the control of the mind. It is a known fact that the human mind has the ability to perceive far more that our conscious awareness lets us know. Subliminal communication is not only used for advertising purposes but for political propaganda and psychological warfare as well, including the use of drugs. It is impressive just how sophisticated this field of activity has become. Whereas intelligence services, both political and commercial, have significant resources dedicated to the development and application of these methods, regrettably the enemy of our souls also exercises its influence over those managing this field.

The methods used are obviously not exposed, neither are they apparent to us, but its results are indeed evident. It is enough to observe pornography, eroticism, and violence in all its forms in television, movies, video, the Internet, and other mass media outlets. Programming could not get more bloody and grotesque. Demonic representations are directly expressed through television programs and films depicting all kinds of satanic beings, vampires (now even "good" ones), aliens, perverts, and malignant personages (including women and children of all ages!)—to the point that this has become sort of "normal." The evil objective behind all this is to attempt to satisfy people's appetite for the flesh and the supernatural, misdirecting their attention to evil rather than to God.

Satan's goal is to contaminate the human mind. Proverbs 23:7 says, *"For as a man thinks within himself, so he is,"* and as he is, so will he act. The Lord has warned us, *"That man ought not to expect that he will receive anything from the Lord, being a double-minded man, unstable in all his ways"* (James 1:7–8). That is why He has admonished us to *"watch over your heart with all diligence"* (Prov. 4:23); God searches the heart. We will not impress nor deceive God with insincere religious rituals, with our prayers just to be heard by others, or with our charitable displays merely to be seen by men. He has said, *"I, the Lord, search the heart, I test the mind, Even to give to each man according to his ways, According to the results of his deeds"* (Jer. 17:10).

Please bear in mind that we must strive for wisdom, even if the evil in the world boasts about knowledge; that we should endeavor to be meek and humble, even if the world admires arrogance; that we should sincerely purpose in our hearts to be loving toward all, even if the ungodly hates everything in your behavior that testifies of God. The Word says, *"To the pure, all things are pure; but to those who are defiled and unbelieving, nothing is pure, but both their mind and their conscience are defiled"* (Titus 1:15).

While in our human perception there appears to be a limit to God's patience toward the agnostic, the unrepentant, the constant evildoer, the Word says, *"What then? If some did not believe, their unbelief will not nullify the faithfulness of God, will it? May it never be! Rather, let God be found true, though every man be found a liar"* (Rom. 3:3-4). Our unbelief does not nullify the faithfulness of God, for God's faithfulness is a result of His loving nature and perfect ways, in which *"there is no variation or shifting shadow"* *(James 1:17).* And so is His faithfulness, for *"if we are faithless, He remains faithful, for He cannot deny Himself"* (2 Tim. 2:13). Let us be thankful to God for His patience and mercy toward us, but let us be equally mindful of His Word, of His warnings and signs. He says, *"Today if you hear His voice, Do not harden your hearts"* (Heb. 3:7-8).

In these later days, the influencing of the mind is a clear sign of this time of deception, for as we have noted earlier, *"our struggle is…against the rulers, against the powers, against the world forces of this darkness, against the spiritual forces of wickedness in the heavenly places"* (Eph. 6:12). Thus, men are reminded:

> *The weapons of our warfare are not of the flesh, but divinely powerful for the destruction of fortresses. We are destroying speculations and every lofty thing raised up against the knowledge of God, and we are taking every thought captive to the obedience of Christ.*
> —2 Corinthians 10:4–5

As for all those that have moved away from God, and for those who have never known Him, here is a word of encouragement for you in these difficult times:

> *In reference to your former manner of life, you lay aside the old self, which is being corrupted in accordance with the lust of deceit, and that you be renewed in the spirit of your mind, and put on the new self, which in the likeness of God has been created in righteousness and holiness of the truth.*
> —Ephesians 4:22–24

Thus, whereas temptation most often comes through the mind, God has given us a free will to do as we choose, which includes our ability to control our mind and direct our thoughts. The Word encourages to do so: *"Finally, brethren, whatever is true, whatever is honorable, whatever is right, whatever is pure, whatever is lovely, whatever is of good repute, if there is any excellence and anything worthy of praise, let your mind dwell on these things"* (Phil. 4:8).

The Surge of Emotionality vs. Spirituality

As we have previously noted, whereas the enemy attacks through the mind, even more so it attacks through the emotions. For man was created with a *spirit*, which makes him in the image of God; with a *soul*, which governs the mind (intelligence and knowledge) and our instincts and emotions under the free will granted to him; and he is also *flesh*, which *"sets its desire against the spirit, and the spirit against the flesh; for these are in opposition to one another, so that you may not do the things that you please"* (Gal. 5:17).

As to the things that pertain to the Spirit of God, a man with a carnal mind cannot understand them, because as noted earlier, they must be discerned through the Spirit. Whereas human knowledge is adequate for the things of this world, wisdom from God is required for the things of the Spirit. So as God is Spirit, *"those who worship Him must worship in spirit and truth"* (John 4:24). Beware that you do not get tangled up with matters of semantics or words, for as noted, *"the letter kills, but the Spirit gives life [revelation]"* (2 Cor. 3:6).

The Spirit gives men multiple gifts, such as to speak in His name, exercise the faith, serve those who He puts in their way, teach the Word, give with humility, lead with devotion, practice mercy with joy, love without hypocrisy, do miracles in His name, and many other gifts as the Spirit wills (Rom. 12:6–9). God also expects us to use those gifts to produce the "fruits" of the Spirit: *"love, joy, peace, patience, kindness, goodness, faithfulness, gentleness, self-control"* (Gal. 5:22-23).

However, in these latter days, as clearly described in 2 Timothy 3:1-5, men have gone stray from God's will, and the following comparison makes this situation evident:

Fruit of the Spirit (Galatians 5:22-23)	Conditions in the Latter Days (2 Timothy 3:1-5)
Love	Unloving, lovers of self, lovers of money
Joy	Lovers of pleasure
Peace	Irreconcilable, treacherous, haters of good, malicious
Patience	Reckless
Kindness	Brutal, ungrateful, conceited
Goodness	Haters of good, unholy
Faithfulness	Revilers, disobedient to parents
Gentleness	Arrogant, boastful
Self-control	Without self-control

Thus, the enemy strives to prevent that the souls of men be placed under the Spirit of God, because then he cannot touch them. For *"all who are being led by the Spirit of God, these are sons of God"* (Rom. 8:14). Conversely, the enemy tempts us through the flesh, *"because the mind set on the flesh is death...is hostile toward God; for it does not subject itself to the law of God, for it is not even able to do so, and those who are in the flesh cannot please God"* (Rom. 8:6-8).

The critical question from the apostle Paul is, *"Wretched man that I am! Who will set me free from the body of this death?"* (Rom. 7:24). It is answered with joy:

> *There is therefore now no condemnation for those who are in Christ Jesus. For the law of the Spirit of life in Christ Jesus has set you free from the law of sin and death. For what the Law could not do, weak as it was in the flesh, God did: sending His own Son in the likeness of sinful flesh and as an offering for sin, He condemned sin in the flesh.*
>
> —ROMANS 8:1–3

Thus, take courage, for even great men of God had to contend with emotions and the flesh, and some were even reprimanded by the Lord. There are many such examples in the Old Testament.

Job

Job is identified in the Scriptures as a man *"blameless, upright, fearing God, and turning away from evil"* (Job 1:1). His integrity, however, was questioned by Satan (in a first sign of rebellion before God) as being the result of God's abundant blessings upon him. The Lord agreed to have Job's integrity be put through a test as a testimony for us, but even when suddenly stripped from his family, wealth, and health, Job did not question God's will: *"The Lord gave and the Lord has taken away. Blessed be the name of the Lord"* (Job 1:21).

Notwithstanding, in the first forty-one chapters of the Book of Job, he recorded his mourning, discouragement, and depressed feelings as he turned his eyes upon himself and his predicament. It was only in chapter 42 that Job came out of his journey of self-pity, repented, and turned his eyes toward God. The Word asserts that as he prayed for his friends he was once again blessed: *"The Lord restored the fortunes of Job when he prayed for his friends, and the Lord increased all that Job had twofold"* (Job 42:10).

The conclusion to Job's story? *"Consider it all joy, my brethren, when you encounter various trials, knowing that the testing of your faith produces endurance. And let endurance have its perfect result, that you may be perfect and complete, lacking in nothing"* (James 1:2–4).

Moses

Moses was the patriarch of the prophets. He led the Israelite people out from their captivity in Egypt.

During their pilgrimage through the Sinai Desert, all suffered severe thirst, which led them to confront Moses and Aaron in a threatening way. Moses sought God's help in prayer, and then He instructed him, *"Take the rod; and you and your brother Aaron assemble the congregation* and speak to the rock *before their eyes, that it may yield its water.... Then Moses lifted up his hand and* struck the rock twice *with his rod; and water came forth abundantly, and the congregation and their beasts drank"* (Num. 20:8, 11, emphasis added). In so doing, Moses disobeyed God, as the Lord had instructed him to speak to the rock, not to strike it (as he did twice). Whether this was the result of fear, given the threatening attitude of the congregation, or an emotional reaction prompted by the desperation of his people, it matters not. God's disappointment was severe because Moses had been blessed to receive the tables with God's Commandments, he had been used by the Almighty to impose upon Egypt the ten plagues which prompted Pharaoh to let the Israelites go, and he was instructed by God to part the Red Sea with his rod, which he did. Therefore, he was no ordinary man. Thus, because to whom much is given, much is required (Luke 12:48), Moses' responsibility was great, and the testimonial significance of his behavior was important before God's people.

The above mishap caused the Lord's judgment upon Moses and Aaron: *"Because you have not believed Me, to treat Me as holy in the sight of the sons of Israel, therefore you shall not bring this assembly into the land which I have given them"* (Num. 20:12). Consequently, Moses saw the Promised Land from a distance but did not enter into it.

The conclusion to Moses' story? *"Do not fear those who kill the body, but are unable to kill the soul; but rather fear Him who is able to destroy both soul and body in hell"* (Matt. 10:28).

Elijah

Elijah the Tishbite (Elias in the New Testament) was an extraordinary prophet of God who He used, among other things, to glorify His name when he confronted Ahab, King of Israel, who was married to Jezebel, a prophetess of Baal. A challenge was made before all of Israel to determine who was the true God, either Baal or the Lord. An offering of one ox was made by the four hundred and fifty prophets of Baal. They killed and placed the remains of the animal over wood at Mount Carmel with no fire under it, and they called on their gods to consume the offering from morning until evening, without anything happening.

Elijah then took twelve stones for each of the tribes of Jacob, built an altar in the name of the Lord, made a large trench around it, and placed the wood and the ox, cut into pieces, on it. He then poured four pitchers of water on the offering and the wood and repeated this three times until the water even filled the trench. Then he called on the Lord to burn it. Fire came from heaven and consumed it all. Then Elijah seized the prophets of Baal and had them slain.

Jezebel then sent word to Elijah, saying, *"So may the gods do to me and even more, if I do not make your life as the life of one of them by tomorrow about this time"* (1 Kings 19:2). And the Word says that Elijah *"was afraid and arose and ran for his life"* (v. 3) into the desert, where he was attended by an angel and went on to have an encounter with God at the Mountain of Horeb. Despite this act of cowardice, the Lord was not finished with Elijah and sent him to anoint Hazael as King over Syria, Jehu as King of Israel, and Elisha as his successor.

What happened to this great man of God?

Elijah was momentarily the victim of fear, an emotion opposite to faith. The Lord has warned us about it: *"Be alert, stand firm in the faith, act like men, be strong"* (1 Cor. 16:13). The Lord, who sees the heart of men, not only forgave him but went on to take Elijah with Him, as described in the Word, in a *"chariot of fire and horses of fire…And Elijah went up by a whirlwind to heaven"* (2 Kings 2:11).

The conclusion to Elijah's story? Even great men of God are subject to fear and the victim of emotions when they do not keep their eyes on Him, the source of their strength.

In the New Testament, other great men of God were also afflicted by emotions and fear.

John the Baptist

The Lord Jesus distinguished John the Baptist, saying, *"This is the one about whom it was written, 'Behold, I send My messenger ahead of You, Who will prepare Your way before You.' Truly, I say to you, among those born of women there has not risen anyone greater than John the Baptist"*

(Matt. 11:10–11). Yet, having baptized the Lord, having seen the heavens open, and having heard the words of the Father saying, *"This is My beloved Son, in whom I am well pleased"* (Matt. 3:16–17), when John was imprisoned by King Herod, a doubt came upon him, and he sent word to Jesus: *"Are You the Expected One, or shall we look for someone else?"* (Matt. 11:2–3). The Lord answered John's messengers in a most loving way: *"Go and report to John the things which you hear and see: the blind receive sight and the lame walk, the lepers are cleansed and the deaf hear, and the dead are raised up, and the poor have the gospel preached to them. And blessed is he who does not take offense at Me"* (Matt. 11:4–6).

The Apostle Peter

Peter was no stranger to emotions. When the Lord Jesus announced His forthcoming death, declaring that, *"You will all fall away, because it is written, 'I will strike down the shepherd, and the sheep shall be scattered'... Peter said to him, 'Even though all may fall away, yet I will not'. And Jesus said to him, 'Truly I say to you, that you yourself shall this very night, before a cock crows twice, shall three times deny Me'"* (Mark 14:27–30). And it all happened just as Jesus foretold him. In fact, all the disciples left Him and fled. I believe that Jesus gave Peter the chance to redeem himself when He appeared to him before His ascension and three times asked Peter whether he loved Him, for the three times that Peter denied Him (John 21:15–17).

The Lord had previously said at Gethsemane, when the disciples could not keep watch for an hour while He waited for Judas and those that were to imprison Him, *"The spirit is willing, but the flesh is weak"* (Mark 14:38). The exhortation of the apostle Paul through the Holy Spirit is clear and affirmative: *"I can do all things through Him who strengthens me"* (Phil. 4:13). And the same is true for all of us who follow Jesus.

The Constraining of Freedom

Whereas the struggle of men for freedom is as ancient as the world itself, in these latter days the trend among nations is toward a world order, a euphemism used to disguise the appetite of the world's hidden powers to gain a firm control over the human race. Satan is obviously behind this, for he promotes wars and infiltrates governments and international political groups; world and regional organizations; scientific and educational entities; and human rights, religious, and mass media institutions with that objective in mind.

Consolidation leads to control, and whereas the rationale for a world order is on the surface appealing and theoretically positive, what satanic forces have in mind is to actually take over the new worldwide power systems once these are set in place, as prophesied. The deceptive arguments used to promote such a worldwide consolidation of power can be seen and read with increasing frequency in today's mass media. A brief review of these arguments includes such points as:

- The world needs a consolidated approach to solve its economic, financial, currency, and trade problems.

- The substitution of physical currencies for electronic currency (*"a mark on his forehead or upon his hand"* [Rev. 14:9]) will offer a safer system against robbery, identity theft, fraud, and as a means to constrain the use of physical currencies by terrorism, narcotic, and mafia organizations.

- Political, social, and religious problems will be portrayed as the cause of world problems, justifying the need for a centralized and unified "guiding force," or a world religion.

- Wars and regional conflicts demand a powerful, centralized and committed world organization to enforce a sustainable peace (unlike the United Nations).

- A fair and equitable distribution of wealth must be implemented, and increasingly large government organizations will be needed to tax the rich and subsidize the poor, and to control social and welfare programs, no matter its effects on the nations' budgets and socio-economic wellbeing.

- Famine in many nations can no longer be allowed to exist, and the new world order will make sure that it is eradicated via controls on prices and production.

- Climate control needs enforcement or the world will become uninhabitable, and this requires stricter global regulations.

In summary, what satanic agents are disguisedly proposing is a new messianic order—the Antichrist—to implement and control a new international system that will allegedly bring peace and prosperity to all the inhabitants in the world! Does it not sound great? Yes, it does—on the surface, as it has been the promise of every dictator through the ages, though the final outcome in each case was to replace men's freedom for tyranny. Jesus, emphasizing to the apostles the selfish and hypocritical nature of men, said, *"For you always have the poor with you"* *(Mark 14:7)*, after a woman anointed Him with an expensive perfume and the apostles criticized her for wasting money that could have been given to the poor.

As noted earlier in this book, men's heart is deceitful and evil and is the cause for the progressive political, social, legal, and ethical deterioration currently prevalent in most fields of human activity. The magnitude of the present world crisis actually stems from the collapse of spiritual values, as mankind has for the most part moved away from God.

This latter-day scenario is the consequence of the abuse of the free will granted to men by God, for which dispensation they will be held responsible and, in due time, judged. This is why God will allow Satan and his evil forces to prevail during the ensuing Great Tribulation period (seven years), testing *"those who dwell upon the earth"* (Rev. 3:10). Thus, the main purpose for this book is to warn all that read it that the hour of judgment is at hand and that it behooves them to seek God's protection.

Consistent with the above developments, the forces of evil are progressively paving the way for the new world order by constraining human freedom in all fields of activity in various and multiple deceptive ways. Whether it is through initiatives to limit the freedom to worship, to exercise one's political and legal rights, to have free access to work and live in peace, to organize in defense of one's legitimate interests, to promote new ideas and initiatives, to enjoy freedom of speech and privacy in their communications, and so on, all such legitimate rights are currently under attack. As noted earlier in these pages, the control of private communications and information through mass media—and the subliminal influence on the mind through the use of technological devices—are factual developments our days.

The CATO Institute is a think tank organization in Washington that represents one of the most prestigious private and independent institutions in the world and whose main objectives are to limit the size of government and to promote free market policies, individual liberty, and peace. In December 2012 the Institute published their annual report titled "Economic Freedom of the World," which addressed the results from surveys conducted in one hundred and forty-four nations of the world to determine their comparative performance with respect to economic freedom based on personal choice, voluntary exchange, and open-market practices. The results from this survey show a clear trend toward the increasing size of governments, its extended influence and control over the private sector, along with the proliferation of norms and restrictions limiting people's freedom of choice. The report says that "the USA, long considered the standard bearer for large industrial nations, shows a significant decline in economic freedom during the last decade."[4] From a ranking of number two—that is, the second most economically free country—in the year 2000, the United States moved to number eight in 2005 and then to number eighteen in 2012. Again, the lower the number, the more economic freedom exists, which means the United States' ranking has decreased over time according to the CATO

Institute's report. Other large nations are not doing much better: Japan now ranks twentieth; Germany, thirty-first; France, forty-seventh; Italy, eighty-third; Mexico, ninety-first; Russia, ninety-fifth; Brazil, one hundred and fifth; China, one hundred and seventh; and India, one hundred and eleventh. The above trend is in line with our contention that the world is clearly moving toward larger government structures and centralized controls in most nations as a way to control and subdue their populations.

It is a statistical fact that economic productivity declines the more that government restrictions put pressure on a nation's freedom to act. The result is lower per capita income, employment, and quality of life. Communist and Socialist nations' socio-economic performance in recent history unequivocally demonstrate this.

From a Christian point of view, I have opted in this writing to focus on personal freedom, on that inner spiritual condition of being unrestrained by the pressures and temptations of this world and by the evil forces that contend with us. However, that does not mean that we can ignore the influence in our lives from those noted external developments and the challenges they present to us. How are we to reinforce our inner peace and faith, which are necessary to enjoy freedom? Jesus Christ gave us some very explicit guidance:

> *If you continue in My word, then you are truly disciples of Mine; and you will know the truth, and the truth will make you free.*
> —JOHN 8:31–32

Let us bear in mind that He Himself is the truth and that wisdom stems from Him.

> *For you were called to freedom, brethren; only do not turn your freedom into an opportunity for the flesh, but through love serve one another.*
> —GALATIANS 5:13

Enjoy in Christ the blessing to be free from sin, to merit His protection, and to be anointed to serve others.

> *The creation itself also will be set free from its slavery to corruption into the freedom of the glory of the children of God.*
> —ROMANS 8:21

This blessing is not apparent to us now, and it most certainly will not be perceivable during the Great Tribulation period that follows, but it will be majestically clear when the Lord Jesus Christ returns to earth in power and glory: *"The lawless one will be revealed whom the Lord will slay with the breath of His mouth and bring to an end by the appearance of His coming"* (2 Thess. 2:8).

The exhortation from this reading is this: *"The Lord will reign forever"* (Ps. 146:10). So do not be deceived, neither confused by the apparent and short-lived prevalence of evil in the world in these latter days, for God is in control and will protect His own. Jesus said, *"In the world you have tribulation, but take courage; I have overcome the world"* (John 16:33). Thus, our sufficiency is in Him and only through Him.

The Manipulation of Fear

The increasing manipulation of fear by evil forces is another external sign of the latter days. (We refer to fear as an emotion opposite to faith and not as a feeling of respect for God and as the beginning of wisdom [Prov. 9:10].)

The power of death, prior to Jesus Christ's first coming to earth, was in the hands of the devil, and he used the fear of death as an emotional pressure point to bring many nations and its people into slavery. This power was taken away from Satan by the Lord Jesus Christ at the cross, so *"that through death He might render powerless him who had the power of death, that is, the devil, and might deliver those who through the fear of death were subject to slavery all their lives"* (Heb. 2:14–15).

Whereas the world has known of murders, assassins, wars and conflicts of all kind through the ages, new fear agents have proliferated in the international scene in these latter days. Terrorist organizations represent a relatively modern version of organized crime, in addition to those mafia organizations of all types and scopes that are still present. These are characterized by extreme brutality, no respect for human life, no rules of engagement and no mercy whatsoever. Their objectives are power and money, no matter how much they may attempt to disguise their true intentions. Their partnerships are equally evil, whether these involve drug and weapon trafficking, money laundering, human slavery, economic or financial corruption, or the like. We all know that this is going on, but what many do not realize is just how extensive and powerful these evil organizations are and to what extent they infiltrate the highest levels of society, both public and private entities and organizations alike.

What does the Word of God say about this unfolding debacle? How can we protect ourselves from it? Let us start with the acknowledgement that Christians are no longer under the power of death, through which power Satan has enslaved so many. To those in Christ, death no longer has dominion over us, for *"He will swallow up death for all time, And the Lord God will wipe tears away from all faces, And He will remove the reproach of His people from all the earth"* (Isa. 25:8).

The reassurance of the Spirit through the apostle Paul is not only comforting but a joyous rebuke of death, when he asserts:

> *But when this perishable will have put on the imperishable, and this mortal will have put on immortality, then will come about the saying that is written, "Death is swallowed up in victory. Oh death, where is your victory? Oh death, where is your sting?"*
> —1 Corinthians 15:54–55

Concerning the fear of death and remembering that God is love, the Scriptures remind us, *"There is no fear in love; but perfect love cast out fear, because fear involves punishment, and the one who fears is not perfected in love"* (1 John 4:18). Thus, our confidence must be predicated on the Lord and His faithfulness toward those that trust Him and believe in Him, for if *"the Lord is for me, I will not fear; What can man do to me?"* (Ps. 118:6).

The Word exhorts us to assume our position in Christ Jesus and to use the authority that He has given to us in His name.

> *For you have not received a spirit of slavery leading to fear again, but you have received a spirit of adoption as sons by which we cry out, "Abba! Father!" The Spirit Himself testifies with our spirit that we are children of God.*
> —Romans 8:15–16

In closing this chapter, and at the risk of sounding like a prophet of doom, there is no denying that we are living in very difficult times. According to Bible prophecies the worst is yet to come for a season, as allowed by God. The validation of this assertion is in the daily news, which covers horror, violence, and massive threats at unprecedented levels, and most everywhere in the world. We all would wish that this trend could be different, by the latter-days prophesies are abundantly clear in this respect and about the period of tribulation that is to follow. However, the good news to those that acknowledge Jesus as the way, the truth, and life is that God's protection is upon them, and they have nothing to fear.

Chapter 5

THE LATTER DAYS AND THE EVENTS TO FOLLOW

ALTHOUGH I HAVE reiterated in prior pages that the main purpose of this book is fundamentally to describe present conditions, portrayed in the Scriptures as the latter days, it is important that after having ascertained where we are we may understand where we are going. I will do so through the description—in as concise and non-controversial fashion as possible—of the coming events prophesied in the Word of God, addressing various interpretations of some of these occurrences but providing scriptural evidence of what the Word of God actually says.

The latter days are presently exposing and portraying conditions that represent a mild precursor of the horrible and devastating events prophesied relative to the Great Tribulation, Satan, the Antichrist, the false prophet, and the war of Armageddon that is to follow and is to be ended by the second coming of the Lord Jesus Christ *"on the clouds of the sky with power and great glory"* (Matt. 24:30).

As to the time of His coming, we have been given the warnings and signs previously described in this book and other Tribulation-related ones that will be addressed later in this book, *"but as to that day and hour no one knows, not even the angels of heaven, nor the Son, but the Father alone"* (Matt. 24:36). The reason for such an incredible level of secrecy is that Satan and his followers actually ignore the date of Jesus' return to Earth, as we do, even though they obviously know that the time is near. Because of this expectation the enemy makes such an effort to confuse and deceive mankind, as prophesied: *"But the Spirit explicitly says that in the later times some will fall away from the faith, paying attention to deceitful spirits and doctrines of demons"* (1 Tim. 4:1).

Chronology of Events

The following summary description of things to come is non-denominational and based on the literal interpretation of the Word of God, which supports the belief that the second coming of Jesus Christ will occur prior to the millennial kingdom of our Lord on Earth, which view was also that of the early Church (through the third century A.D.), and which a great and increasing number of bible scholars and interpreters support today.

The Rapture

The word *rapture* is derived from the Koine Greek *harpagisometha,* which means "caught up" or "taken away," and from the Latin Vulgate *rapio,* which similarly means "to catch up" or "take away." This doctrine spouses that after the latter days addressed in this book and prior to the Tribulation period, the true and holy Christian church will be removed from Earth by the Lord. He will do so according to His promises, and to spare mankind from the hour of trial that is about to come upon those who have not believed in the Lord Jesus Christ or have opposed Him following Satan's deception. As noted in 1

Thessalonians 4:16-17: *"For the Lord Himself will descend from heaven with a shout, with the voice of the archangel and with the trumpet of God, and the dead in Christ shall rise first. Then we who are alive and remain will be caught up together with them in the clouds to meet the Lord in the air, and so we shall always be with the Lord."* This promise is concordant with many other key scriptures in the Old and the New Testament, as follows:

> *Now at that time Michael, the great prince who stands guard over the sons of your people, will arise. And together will be a time of distress such as never occurred since there was a nation until that time; and at that time your people, everyone who is found written in the book,* will be rescued.
> —DANIEL 12:1, EMPHASIS ADDED

> *For as in those days before the flood…came and took them away, so will the coming of the Son of Man be. Then there shall be two men in the field; one will be taken, and one will be left. Two women will be grinding at the mill;* one will be taken, and one will be left.
> —MATTHEW 24:38-41, EMPHASIS ADDED

> *Behold, I tell you a mystery; we shall not all sleep, but we shall all be changed, in a moment, in the twinkling of an eye, at the last trumpet; for the trumpet will sound,* and the dead will be raised imperishable, and we will be changed.
> —1 CORINTHIANS 15:51-52, EMPHASIS ADDED

This "last trumpet" is for the *gathering* of the dead in Christ and is not a trumpet of judgment, as described in Revelation 8 and 9.

> *And to wait for His Son from heaven, whom He raised from the dead, that is Jesus,* who delivers us *from the wrath to come.*
> —1 THESSALONIANS 1:10, EMPHASIS ADDED

> For God has not destined us for wrath, *but for obtaining salvation through our Lord Jesus Christ.*
> —1 THESSALONIANS 5:9, EMPHASIS ADDED

Revelation 3:10, previously referred to in this book, assures all those who *"have kept the word of My perseverance, [that] I also will keep you [other translations use the word "spare you"] from the hour of testing, that hour which is about to come upon the whole world, to test those who dwell upon the earth".*

As God spared Lot and his family from the destruction of Sodom and Gomorrah (Gen. 18–19), raptured Enoch to Heaven before the Flood (Gen. 5:24), and saved Noah and his family (Gen. 7:7) from it, so will He rescue the true Christian church from the Tribulation wrath and divine judgment. It will not fall on the body of Christ, whose saints are indwelled by the Holy Spirit, as reiterated by irrefutable scriptures:

> *Do not let your heart be troubled; believe in God, believe also in Me. In My Father's house are many dwelling places; if it were not so, I would have told you; for I go to prepare a place for you. If I go and prepare a place for you,* I will come again, and receive you to Myself; *that where I am, there you may be also.*
> —JOHN 14:1–3, EMPHASIS ADDED

Clearly, Jesus speaks of receiving the church (lifting it up) and not of descending to Earth, as in His second coming, in great power and glory. Evidently, these are two separate events.

> *Therefore there is* now no condemnation *for those who are in Christ Jesus.*
> —ROMANS 8:1, EMPHASIS ADDED

> *And to wait for His Son from Heaven, whom He raised from the dead, that is Jesus,* who delivers us from the wrath to come.
> —1 THESSALONIANS 1:10, EMPHASIS ADDED

> *But He, having offered* one sacrifice for sins for all time, *sat down at the right hand of God, waiting from that time onward until His enemies be made a footstool for His feet.*
> —HEBREWS 10:12–13, EMPHASIS ADDED

Thus, Jesus Christ—and the church that He is the head of—cannot ever be made the subject of reproach or subjected to the wrath of God, as the Lord told Judas Thaddaeus: *"Jesus answered and said to him, 'If anyone loves Me, he will keep My word; and My Father will love him, and We will come to him, and make Our abode with him'"* (John 14:23).

For that very reason, Christ bestowed upon His church the Holy Spirit, who *"will guide you into all the truth"* (John 16:13). And when the Holy Spirit is removed from earth prior to the Tribulation (as commented below), the church that He indwells will be also removed with Him.

> *Do you not know that you are the temple of God and that the Spirit of God dwells in you?*
> —1 CORINTHIANS 3:16

The enemy cannot touch the true church, for it is the body of Christ, indwelled by the Holy Spirit.

Notice that nowhere in the Old Testament is the church mentioned relative to the Great Tribulation period (Deut. 4:29–30; Jer. 30:4–11; Dan. 8:24–27, 12:1–2); neither in the New Testament is the church addressed in connection with it, only Israel, and everyone who did not accept the truth testified by the Lord Jesus Christ to them.

The messages to the church in Revelation 1 through 3 stop short of the opening by the Lamb of the seven seals in Revelation 6, and it is not mentioned again in the following chapters concerning the Tribulation period. This is simply so because the church will no longer be on Earth but with God.

Who will remain on Earth to face the wrath of God? All those who will not believe in Christ Jesus, both Jews and gentiles, along with those who will follow after Satan's designs, ungrateful and unholy, who will commit all kinds of wicked and evil deeds, who will never accept the truth or the salvation freely offered to them by the Lord.

However, before the Great Tribulation comes, the Lord will extend one more chance to repent, *"for the Lord is not slow about His promise, as some count slowness, but is patient toward you, not wishing for any to perish but for all to come to repentance"* (2 Pet. 3:9). Further, He promised: *"And this gospel of the kingdom shall be preached in the whole world as a testimony to all the nations, and then the end will come"* (Matt. 24:14). Therefore, take heed of what the Lord says: *"'At the acceptable time I listened to you, and on the day of salvation I helped you.' Behold, now is 'the acceptable time,' behold, now is 'the day of salvation'"* (2 Cor. 6:2).

> For... [God] has granted to us His precious and magnificent promises, so that by them you might become partakers of the divine nature, having escaped the corruption that is in the world by lust.
> —2 Peter 1:4

The Rapture is a most important future event for the true church of Christ, for those that uphold His Word and follow His example. We have been promised that *"the dead in Christ will raise first. Then we* [the church] *who are alive and remain will be* caught up *together with them in the clouds to meet the Lord in the air, and so we shall always be with the Lord"* (1 Thess. 4:16, emphasis added). This is not to be confused with the Lord's second coming, which is to follow; then *He will come down* to Earth: *"In that day His feet will stand on the Mount of Olives"* (Zech. 14:4).

The Rapture will be a sudden event. First Corinthians 15:52 tells us that *"in a moment, in the twinkling of an eye... the dead will be raised imperishable, and we will be changed."* Even if labeled by Paul a mystery, there will be nothing secret about it, as some have referred to it. Most certainly it will be evident to all.

The Rapture is not a recent doctrine, as some have misrepresented it, but it was the subject of a sermon titled "On the Last Times, the Antichrist, and the End of the World," delivered by Pseudo-Ephraem, a Byzantine leader, over one thousand four hundred years ago. It became a popular doctrine but was later ignored during ensuing centuries, reacquiring significance in the seventeenth century as Bible reading gained momentum.

The Rapture is a blessed scriptural promise for the true believers, one given to us so we may "comfort one another"

(1 Thess. 4:18) and to encourage the faithful: *"Therefore, my beloved brethren, be steadfast, immovable, always abounding in the work of the Lord, knowing that your toil is not in vain in the Lord"* (1 Cor. 15:58).

I do not wish to omit the fact that there are Bible interpreters that believe that the Rapture will take place in the middle of the Tribulation period ("mid-Tribulationists") and others who advocate that it will occur at the end of the Tribulation ("late-wrath" interpreters), but their scriptural support is weak. Lastly, there are those that support the post-Tribulation position, which places the Rapture after the Tribulation period, which they define as the entire present age, prior to the second coming of Christ.

The Removal of the Constrainer

The removal of the constrainer is also one of the most important events of the latter days, as addressed in 2 Thessalonians 2:6–8:

> *And you know what restrains him now, so in his time he might be revealed. For the mystery of lawlessness is already at work; only he [the Holy Spirit] who now restrains will do so until he is taken out of the way. Then the lawless one will be revealed whom the Lord will slay with the breath of His mouth and bring to an end by the appearance of His coming.*

The removal of the Holy Spirit from Earth will have enormous consequences. In the first place, it will be simultaneous with the Rapture of the true church of Christ, as righteous believers are the temple of the Holy Spirit and will leave the Earth along with Him. Secondly, the absence of the Holy Spirit, who was appointed by Jesus Christ to "*teach [us] all things, and to bring to your remembrance all that I said to you*" (John 14:26), will facilitate the deception of evil during the Tribulation period that is to follow.

The removal of the Holy Spirit from Earth—concurrent with the casting down of Satan and his angels to it and the dispensation given to the latter during the second half of the Tribulation period to prevail over the Jewish people and unbelievers outside the true church—will represent the last call to salvation (and the supreme test) for them. For those who previously rejected Christ's salvation, in order to gain it during the Tribulation period they will have to face devastating conditions and, for the most part, martyrdom. However, they will become a *"great multitude"* (Rev. 7:9).

The Great Tribulation Period

This worldwide development was referred to by Christ Himself *"as the great tribulation, such as has not occurred since the beginning of the world until now, nor ever shall"* (Matt. 24:21). This period will last seven years, as prophesied by Daniel 9 and 12, and at the beginning of its first three and a half years the Antichrist will make his appearance. He is *"the man of lawlessness...the son of destruction, who opposes and exalts himself above every so-called god or object of worship, so that he takes his seat in the temple of God, displaying himself as being God"* (2 Thess. 2:3-4). This incredible profanity was addressed by Jesus: *"Therefore, when you see the abomination of desolation which was spoken of through Daniel the prophet, standing in the holy place (let the reader understand), then those who are in Judea must flee to the mountains"* (Matt. 24:15-16).

The Antichrist and the False Prophet

This desecration will be followed by the second Beast's abomination (that of the *false prophet*). He will force everyone to make an image of the Antichrist and set it in the holy of holies, and through Satan's deception he will give it the ability to look alive (Dan. 12:11; Rev. 13:11–15). This will only become possible because *"it was given to him* [the dragon, or Satan]*... authority to act for forty-two months.... It was also given to him to make war with the saints and to overcome them"* (Rev. 13:5, 7).

The Antichrist will attempt to impersonate the Lord Jesus Christ, but he will be exposed for what he will be: the exact opposite. As Satan aspires to be like God the Father, he will display the Antichrist as the "savior of a troubled world," as the "real Messiah," for which purpose he will vest him with his power and authority *"and will show great signs and wonders, so as to mislead, if possible, even the elect [the Jews and the Tribulation saints]"* (Matt. 24:24). That fake "trinity" will be completed by the false prophet, the second Beast. Some of these displays will be *"false wonders, and with the deception of wickedness for those who perish"* (2 Thess. 2:9–10).

Following is a description of the Antichrist, the "son" of Satan, or the first Beast, as described by the Scriptures and as compared with Jesus Christ:

	Jesus	The Antichrist, or Beast
Origin	the Son of God; came from Heaven to save all those that believe in Him (John 3:16)	will come from the abyss to do Satan's will (Rev. 17:8)

Profile	loved us first and gave His life at the cross as a ransom for many (Matt. 20:28)	hates men as God's creation and will came to deceive, to kill, and to destroy (Rev. 13:14–15)
Personality	meek and humble; He did not regard equality with God as a thing to be grasped, and became obedient to the point of death at the cross (Phil. 2:6–8)	will be boastful and blasphemous before God and His tabernacle (those who dwell in heaven). (Rev. 13:6)
Goal	purposed to save mankind for love and for the glory of God (Titus 2:11)	pursues the worship of Satan, bringing glory to himself (Rev. 13:3–4)
Approach	respects the free-will granted to men (Gal. 5:13–16)	will lead by oppression and submission and will make war with the Jews and the Tribulation saints (Rev. 13:7)
Scope	leads men to a spiritual, loving, and eternal relationship with God (John 17:20–24)	desires to rule the Earth and to be worshiped by those who dwell in it (Rev. 13:8), claiming to be God (2 Thess. 2:4)
Veracity	came to give testimony of the truth, for He is the truth (John 14:6)	a liar like Satan, the very representation of evil, as well as a faker, a counterfeiter, and a "smooth talker" (Dan. 11:32)
Kingdom	Jesus' kingdom will last forever (Isa. 9:7).	The Beast's kingdom will last three and a half years, or the second half of the Tribulation period (Rev. 13:5).

| Destiny | will reign forever in the kingdom of God (Luke 1:32–33) | already condemned and will be thrown alive and forever into the lake of fire, along with the false prophet (Dan. 7:11; Rev. 19:20; 20:10) |

The Antichrist, to whom the dragon will give "his throne" (Rev. 13:2), will be a man of extraordinary intellect, political savvy, leadership conditions, charisma, and popularity, as well as a military genius. But at the same time he will be essentially satanic (thoroughly like his mentor), evil, boastful, arrogant, destructive, and the embodiment of everything that is opposed to God.

Peace Treaty with Israel

At the outset of the seven-year Tribulation period, the Antichrist will drive world attention to himself by signing a peace treaty with Israel, an elusive development sought out by so many world leaders in recent years (Dan. 9:27; Ezek. 38:8). Thus, many Jews will rejoice and look at him as the real Messiah prophesied, having failed to recognize Jesus Christ at His first coming (John 1:11). However, Isaiah 28:18 prophesied about this covenant, saying, *"Your covenant with death shall be canceled* [sic]*, And your pact with Sheol will not stand,"* as in fact will happen.

The Rebuilding of the Temple

The Beast will cause the Jewish temple to be rebuilt in Jerusalem: *"It will be built again...even in times of distress"* (Dan. 9:25). This is reaffirmed by Jesus Christ himself in Matthew 24:15: *"Therefore, when you see the abomination of desolation which was spoken of through Daniel the prophet, standing in the holy place."*. Also, in 2 Thessalonians 2:3–4 we read, *"The son of destruction, who opposes and exalts himself above every so-called god or object of worship, so that he takes his seat in the temple of God, displaying himself as being God."* The rebuilt temple is also mentioned in Revelation 11:1.

The Ten Kingdoms

The Antichrist will cause ten kings to unite *"who have not yet received a kingdom, but they receive authority as kings with the beast for one hour. These have one purpose, and they give their power and authority to the beast. These will wage war against the Lamb, and the Lamb will overcome them, because He is Lord of lords and King of kings, and those who are with Him are the called and chosen and faithful"* (Rev. 17:12–14). Many Bible scholars consider these kingdoms to be the reemergence of the old Roman Empire, a mixture *"partly of iron and partly of pottery"* (Dan. 2:42), representing some strong and some weaker nations. This assumption is a strong probability. But the world today is reorganizing along economic, political, and religious groups of countries, and these could become new so-called kingdoms (nations) under the Antichrist. However, this is not a critical point, as we have been already foretold that the Beast will be given authority to rule over the whole world for three and a half years, during the latter part of the Tribulation period (Rev. 13:4–5, 15–18).

The Judgments of God

It should be clear to the reader that God's hour of trial is directed toward men in rebellion against Him, inasmuch as Satan, the Antichrist and the false prophet have already been judged. These judgments are manifested in chronological, successive order, increasing in frequency and intensity, just as the birth pangs prophesied in the

Word (Matt. 24:8; 1 Thess. 5:3). The seal judgments will be released first, followed by the trumpets, and then, in rapid succession, by the bowls.

The reading of these judgments strikes fear in those who are uncertain about their relationship with God, and the natural reaction is to put aside that which frightens us. Do not do it, for heeding a warning is always a blessing. Rather, enter through prayer into the realm of the supernatural, and God will uplift you and give you wisdom, peace, and courage.

Awareness about these judgments should help you understand what is at stake for the human race in general and for those who will go through them in particular. Whereas in the greatest act of sacrificial love ever given to the world Jesus Christ opened the way to the eternal kingdom of God for all who believe in Him, rejection represents the greatest offense ever to stem from the heart of men. Essentially, this is what is at stake, and men will be judged according to their own free choices.

This is why it is worth repeating the words of the Spirit through John: *"Blessed is he who reads and those who hear the words of the prophecy, and heed the things which are written in it; for the time is near"* (Rev. 1:3).

The Seven Seals

Revelation chapters 6, 7 and 8 address the Lamb's opening of the seven seals during the first half on the Tribulation period (three and a half years), releasing the four horses of the Apocalypse with authority over one-fourth of the earth:

- The white horse of conquest: *"And he who sat on it [the Antichrist] had a bow; and a* crown was given to him; and he went out conquering, and to conquer" (Rev. 6:2).

- The red horse of war: *"And to him who sat on it was granted to take peace from the Earth, and that men should slay one another, and a great sword was given to him"* (Rev. 6:4).

- The black horse of famine: *"With a pair of scales in his hand"* (Rev. 6:5–6).

- The ashen horse of death, followed by Hades: *"And authority was given to them over a fourth of the Earth, to kill with sword and with famine and with pestilence and by wild beasts of the Earth"* (Rev. 6:8).

It also reveals that when the sixth seal is opened, there will be a great earthquake, the sun will turn black, and the moon will become like blood. The sky is to be split like a scroll, with every mountain and island moving out of their places (Rev. 6:12–14). And the people of the earth will then understand that God reigns, that His repeated pleas and warnings over thousands of years were sadly ignored, and that judgment toward evil and ungodly people has finally come.

And the kings of the earth and the great men and the commanders and the rich and the strong and every slave and free man hid themselves in the caves and among the rocks of the mountains; and they said to the mountains and the rocks, "Fall on us and hide us from the presence of Him who sits on the throne, and

from the wrath of the Lamb; for the great day of His wrath has come; and who is able to stand?"
—REVELATION 6:15–17

After these revelations, the seventh seal will bring about total stillness, with *"the four angels standing at the four corners of the earth, holding back the four winds on the earth, so that no wind should blow on the earth or on the sea or on any tree"* (Rev. 7:1).

This great stillness will usher the appearance of the Jewish preachers, as noted below. Revelation 8:1 says that *"there was silence in heaven for about half an hour."* What a chilling and frightening experience this will be! Absolute stillness and silence, like the calm that precedes the storm. It is a pause for meditation prior to the actual unleashing of the wrath of God, as depicted and executed through the trumpet and bowl punishments.

The 144,000 Jewish Preachers

This unique group of Jewish bond-servants, twelve thousand from each of the tribes of Israel (except the tribe of Dan because of idolatry), were chosen by God and sealed in their foreheads with the name of the Lamb and of His Father (Rev. 14:1). They will have God's protection to preach His Word to Jews and Gentiles going through the Tribulation.

The four angels holding the winds at the four corners of the Earth were told, *"Do not harm the earth or the sea or the trees, until we have sealed the bond-servants of our God in their foreheads"* (Rev. 7:3). They were accredited to bring salvation to *"a great multitude, which no one could count, from every nation and all tribes and peoples and tongues, standing before the throne and before the Lamb, clothed with white robes, and palm branches were in their hands;*

and they cry out with a loud voice, saying, 'Salvation to our God who sits on the throne, and to the Lamb'" (Rev. 7:9–10).

This extraordinary group of Jewish preachers will come to take over the evangelistic role of the true Christian church, taken away by the Lord prior to the Tribulation. Their missionary quest will be heroic and courageous, as conditions on Earth will be horrendous. Their effort will be greatly rewarded:

> *And I looked, and behold, the Lamb was standing on the Mount Zion, and with Him one hundred and forty-four thousand, having His name and the name of His Father written on their foreheads. And I heard a voice from heaven, like the sound of many waters and like the sound of loud thunder, and the voice which I heard was like the sound of harpists playing on their harps. And they sang a new song before the throne and before the four living creatures and the elders, and no one could learn the song except the one hundred and forty-four thousand who had been purchased from the earth. These are the ones who have not been defiled with women, for they have kept themselves chaste. These are the ones who follow the Lamb wherever He goes. These have been purchased from among men as first fruits to God and to the Lamb. And no lie was found in their mouth; they are blameless.*
> —REVELATION 14:1–5

The Casting of Satan from Heaven

The revolt in heaven of Satan and his angels, waging war against Michael and his angels loyal to God, is described in Revelation 12:7–13. It culminates with the casting out of Satan to Earth, along with his fallen angels, as commented earlier in this book. The impact from this event will gravitate on Satan's efforts to center his struggle against God's elect, the people of Israel. The true church will no longer be on Earth, and those who did not follow Christ will still need to mend ways with the Lord, in the process becoming Tribulation saints.

The Antichrist Breaks His Covenant with Israel

Daniel 9:27 reveals that *"he will make a firm covenant with the many for one week [seven years], but in the middle of the week he will put a stop to sacrifice and grain offering; and on the wing of abominations will come one who makes desolate, even until a complete destruction, one that is decreed, is poured out on the one who makes desolate."* This is the precursor of the Antichrist's attack on Israel.

Gog and Magog Invade Israel

During the first half of the Tribulation period, the Antichrist convinces several nations, collectively addressed as the "King of the North" (Dan. 11:40)—for the nations involved are to the north of Israel—to invade Israel. This is addressed in Ezekiel 38 and 39, where we find:

- "Gog" means "end-time ruler", while the "land of Magog" stands for Russia, "Meshech" for Moscow, and "Tubal" for Siberia.

- Persia stands for Iran and Iraq (one historical origin), Libya, Ethiopia, Gomer (today's Germany), and Togarmah (Turkey and Syria combined).

- The "King of the South," who is to join this invasion, as noted in Daniel 11:40, is identified as Egypt, frequently referred to in Scripture as the "land to the south."

- This northern invasion alliance *"will come like a storm; you will be like a cloud covering the land, you and all your troops, and many peoples with you"* (Ezek. 38:9). And the Lord further asserts, *"It shall come about in the last days that I will bring you against My land, in order that the nations may know Me when I am sanctified through you before their eyes, O Gog"* (Ezek. 38:16).

The northern invasion was also identified by the prophet Isaiah: *"And the Assyrian will fall by a sword not of man, And a sword not of man will devour him"* (Isa. 31:8). The destruction of more than 80 percent of the invading force (only one-sixth will survive and flee back to the north) will be brought about by the Lord through a *"great earthquake...the mountains will also be thrown down, the steep paths will collapse and every wall will fall to the ground...Every man's sword will be against his brother. With pestilence and with blood I shall enter into judgment with him; and I will rain on him, and on his troops, and on the many peoples that are with him, a torrential rain, with hailstones, fire and brimstone"* (Ezek. 38:19–22).

It is noteworthy that the plotting of the northern invasion against Israel will only encounter protests by *"Sheba and Dedan* [Arab countries] *and the merchants of Tarshish, with all its villages* [English speaking nations]" as they accuse the invaders of their intention *"to carry away silver and gold, to take away cattle and goods, to capture great spoil"* (Ezek. 38:13) but offer no further evidence of involvement in the conflict! This seems incomprehensible if notice is not taken of God's purposes in the handling of this situation. His purposes surely include such intentions as:

1. To chastise Israel for entering into a treaty with the Antichrist instead of seeking God's help (Isa. 28:18). The Lord had already promised that *"He will deliver us from the Assyrian"* (Mic. 5:5), but Israel paid no attention to God's promise. The reference to the Assyrian is because God had in times past used it as His Rod against Israel's disobedience.

2. To inflict a devastating defeat on the forces of evil and the Antichrist at the mountains of Israel (Ezek. 39:1–5), as a testimony to Israel and to all nations of the world that *God reigns, and that He is in control.* It took the remnant of Israel seven months to dispose of the dead and seven years to clean up the war debris (Ezek. 39:9–12).

3. As a warning to all nations. This is not to be confused by the dispensation that He would grant Satan, the Antichrist, and the false prophet in the near future, and for the period of forty-two months, when they would be allowed *"to make war with the saints and to overcome them; and authority over every tribe and people and tongue and*

> *nation was given to him. And all that dwell upon the Earth will worship him, every one whose name has not been written from the foundation of the world in the book of life of the Lamb who has been slain. If anyone has an ear, let him hear"* (Rev. 13:7–9). Nevertheless, this defeated invasion will be an event on the way to the final day of reckoning, during which time the trumpets and bowls of God's judgment will truly shake up the world, culminating with the war of Armageddon, when evil forces will be destroyed and the Antichrist and the false prophet thrown alive into the lake of fire. At this time Satan will be locked up in the abyss for one thousand years (the Millennium), upon the Lord's second coming.

There are Bible commentators who believe that the invasion of Israel from the north has actually happened in centuries past, but this is not supported by Scriptures that refer to this invasion during the *"later years"* (Ezek. 38:8) and to Israel as a nation, which was not the case before the present time.

There are others who believe that the northern invasion will be part of the war of Armageddon at the end of the Tribulation period, just before the second coming of the Lord, but these are separate events, as will be addressed later in this book.

The Antichrist Occupation of Palestine

With the defeat of the northern confederacy at the hands of the Lord, the world will enter into a period of great confusion. One of the world's great coalitions will have been decimated, which will tilt the balance of power toward the descendants of the former Roman Empire: the European Federation, dominated by the Antichrist. This time of transition is prophesied in Psalm 2:1-2: *"Why are the nations in an up roar, And the peoples devising a vain thing? The kings of the earth take their stand, And the rulers take counsel together against the Lord and against His Anointed."* The Antichrist will take advantage of this situation, and *"he will go forth with great wrath to destroy and annihilate many. He will pitch the tents of his royal pavilion between the seas and the beautiful Holy Mountain; yet he will come to his end, and no one will help him"* (Dan. 11:45).

The Antichrist's False Death

The Antichrist will reach the pinnacle of his power and dominance when, after appearing to have been killed, his apparent fatal wound will be healed. This is a gross misrepresentation of the death and resurrection of Jesus Christ. Revelation 13:3-4 states, *"And I saw one of his heads* [seven, according to Revelation 13:1] *as if it had been slain, and his fatal wound was healed. And the whole earth was amazed and followed the beast"* (emphasis added). This point is worth a careful analysis. Some Bible interpreters consider it possible that the Antichrist was in fact killed because the same word "slain" (*plégê*) used above was the one used to described Jesus' death (Rev. 5:6). However, when used in the aforementioned scripture it referred to a vision of "the Lamb standing, *as if slain,*" not actually slain, which coincides with the fake death of the Antichrist. Further, the word *plégê* actually means "wound, blow," and "only metaphorically denotes a mortal wound inflicted on the satanic beast in Revelation 13:3."[5]

Some interpreters commenting on the presumed resurrection of the Antichrist by Satan note that such an event could have been based on the authority that God gave him for forty-two months to test (defeat) the Tribulation saints during that period. However, this writer believes that not to be the case, as life *is* Christ, and that prerogative pertains only to Him (John 14:6: *"I am the way, and the truth, and life"*). Moreover, Jesus Christ stated His authority over life in a very plain and clear way when He said, *"For this reason the Father loves Me, because I lay down My life that I might take it again. No one has taken it away from Me, but I lay it down on my own, and I have authority to take it up again"* (John 10:17–18).

Also, note that in Revelation 13:3, John states, *"I saw one of his heads* [out of seven] *as if slain"* (emphasis added), which in my view it does not denote any certainty of death but the appearance of it.

The Abomination of Desolation

This event will the turning point of the Tribulation period, beginning the second half of it, which will last 1,290 days (three and a half years), as per Daniel 12:11. That sacrilegious abomination will unleash the power of God's wrath like never before.

The Antichrist, encouraged by the staggering effect on the whole world of his apparent resurrection and in pursuit of his objective to emulate Jesus Christ, will present himself as the Messiah, abolish the regular sacrifice, and *"take his seat in the temple of God, displaying himself as being God"* (2 Thess. 2:4).

With the support of the false prophet, *"who deceives those who dwell on the earth because of the signs which it was given him to perform in the presence of the beast, telling those who dwell on the earth to make an image of the beast who had the wound of the sword and has come to life. And there was given to him to give breath to the image of the beast, that the image of the beast would even speak and cause as many as do not worship the image of the beast to be killed"* (Rev. 13:14–15).

With the above false displays of deity, power, signs, and wonders, without the Holy Spirit and the church on Earth to enlighten the masses, deception and confusion will overtake most of the world.

The Antichrist Will Rule the World

Satan will be behind the political, economic, social, and religious takeover of the entire world by the Antichrist during the second half of the Tribulation period, under the time dispensation given to him by God: *"And there was given to him a mouth speaking arrogant words and blasphemies; and authority to act for forty-two months was given to him"* (Rev. 13:5).

Politically no group or individual will be in a position to antagonize him without exposing itself/himself to be destroyed or killed except the 144,000 Jewish preachers protected by God's mark. The Antichrist will have a demonic network that will greatly exceed the combined forces of all the secret service organizations in the world, which will end up working for him anyway. It should be remembered that, under the authority given by God to Satan during the second half of the Tribulation period, which he will transfer on to the Antichrist, the world will proclaim, *"Who is like the beast, and who is able to wage war with him?"* (Rev. 13:4). Moreover, *"It was given to him to make war with the saints and to overcome them; and authority over every tribe and people and tongue and nation was given to him"* (Rev. 13:7).

Economically he will centralize and exercise control over all economic, commercial, and financial systems worldwide, creating one *"that causes all, the small and the great, and the rich and the poor, and the freemen and the slaves, to be given a mark on their right hand or in their forehead, and he provides that no one should be able to buy or to sell, except the one who has the mark, either the name of the beast or the number of his name. Here is wisdom. Let him who has understanding calculate the number of the beast, for the number is that of a man; and his number is six hundred and sixty six"* (Rev. 13:16–18).

Clearly, this dictatorial control system will be intended as a countermeasure to the protection that will be extended by God to the 144,000 Jewish preachers during the last portion of the Tribulation period, along with the faithful remnant of messianic Jews that God will protect at Petra and the surviving Tribulation saints.

Currencies, and even gold and silver, will no longer function as a means of payment, for without the mark of the Beast, no one will be able to buy or sell.

Religiously, the deception promoted by the Antichrist and the false prophet will be such that in the words of the Lord Jesus Christ: *"Unless those days had been cut short, no life would have been saved; but for the sake of the elect those days shall be cut short"* (Matt. 24:22).

The nations, except for the remnant of Israel and the Tribulation saints, will actually believe that the Antichrist, who apparently died and was resurrected by Satan, and who fights against Christ for a new world order, is in fact the Messiah. This will usher in a new universal religion allowing men to be free to do whatever they please and where compassion will be replaced by power and love for pleasure.

The Antichrist, who will enter the temple in Jerusalem and will declare himself to be God (as noted above), will accompany his claim with great signs and wonders:

> [His] coming is in accord with the activity of Satan, with all power and signs and false wonders, and with all the deception of wickedness for those who perish, because they did not receive the love of the truth so as to be saved. For this reason God will send upon them a deluding influence so that they might believe what is false, in order that they all may be judged who did not believe the truth, but took pleasure in wickedness.
> —2 THESSALONIANS 2:9–12

It will be recalled that *"all that dwell upon the earth will worship him, everyone whose name has not been written from the foundation of the world in the book of life of the Lamb who has been slain"* (Rev. 13:8).

The Tribulation saints who refuse to receive the mark of the Beast will most likely die in martyrdom, as noted in Revelation 20:4: *"And I saw the souls of those who had been beheaded because of the testimony of Jesus and because of the word of God, and those who had not worshiped the beast or his image, and had not received the mark upon their foreheads and upon their hand; and they came to life and reigned with Christ for a thousand years."* Regrettably, that means that the rest who will worship the Antichrist and receive his mark will relinquish their eternal salvation.

> *If anyone worships the beast and his image, and receives a mark on his forehead or upon his hand, he also will drink of the wine of the wrath of God, which is mixed in full strength in the cup of His anger; and he will be tormented with fire and brimstone in the presence of the holy angels and in the presence of the Lamb.*
> —REVELATION 14:9–10

The Antichrist will be aided by the second Beast, the false prophet, who *"makes the earth and those who dwell in it to worship the first beast [the antichrist], whose fatal wound was healed. And he performs great signs, so that he even makes fire come down out of heaven to the earth in the presence of men"* (Rev. 13:12–13).

The false prophet will be a great deceiver who will look like a religious man and have the appearance of a lamb, but he will speak words of death: *"And I saw another beast coming up out of the earth; and he had two horns like a lamb and he spoke as a dragon"* (Rev. 13:11). He will be the leader of the new world religion created to worship the Antichrist as God.

The Two Witnesses

The role and ministry of these two witnesses, to be sent by God to warn Israel, are addressed in Revelation 11:3–14 but not their identity.

Verse 3 tells us, *"And I will grant authority to my two witnesses, and they will prophesy for twelve hundred and sixty days, clothed in sackcloth."* That means that they will be direct messengers from God who will carry out their ministry at a time of apostasy during the second half of the Tribulation period and before the coming of the Lord, just as John the Baptist did before the Lord's first coming. The fact that they will be dressed in sackcloth as John the Baptist did, and as most prophets of old did, reaffirms their ministry as one of judgment and their call a plea to repentance.

Verse 4 says, *"These will be the two olive trees and the two lampstands that stand before the Lord on the earth."* This is just as prophesied by Zechariah 4:11, 14: *"Then I asked [the angel] and said to him: 'What are these two olive trees on the right of the lampstand and on its left?'... Then he said: 'These are the two anointed ones, who are standing by the Lord of the whole earth.'"* Revelation 11:5 adds, *"And if anyone wants to harm them, fire proceeds out of their mouth and devours their enemies; so if anyone would desire to harm them, in this manner he must be killed."* They will be protected by God for a season, until the completion of their ministry, as Christ was.

In Revelation 11:6 we read, *"These have the power to shut up the sky, so that rain may not fall during the days of their prophesying; and they have the power over the waters to turn them into blood, and to smite the earth with every plague, as often as they desire."* Signs from God concerning rain, and for the same length of time, were given to Elijah in his days (1 Kings 17:1); and regarding pestilences and turning the water into blood, these were signs given to Moses (among other signs) to force Pharaoh to let Israel be freed from slavery in Egypt (Exod. 7–9).

> *When they have finished their testimony, the beast that comes up out of the abyss will make war with them, and overcome them and kill them. And their*

> *dead bodies will lie in the street of the great city which mystically is called Sodom and Egypt, where also their Lord was crucified. Those from the peoples and tribes and tongues and nations will look at their dead bodies for three and a half days, and will not permit their dead bodies to be laid in a tomb. And those who dwell on the earth will rejoice over them and celebrate; and they will send gifts to one another, because these two prophets tormented those who dwell on the earth.*
> —REVELATION 11:7–10

These scriptures depict the spiritual drama of those who ignore God's Word, as well as the warnings and pleas of His messengers, and take temporary pleasure indulging in ungodly and evil lives under the false notion that God does not exist or that He does not care.

When confronted with those who testify to the truth and require repentance from them, they hate them for it and even rejoice when those messengers are silenced, persecuted, or even killed.

But this time the two witnesses will be raised by God from the dead before their very eyes: *"But after the three and a half days, the breath of life from God came into them, and they stood on their feet; and great fear fell upon those who were watching them. And they heard a loud voice from heaven saying to them, 'Come up here.' Then they went up into heaven in the cloud, and their enemies watched them. And in that hour there was a great earthquake, and a tenth of the city fell; seven thousand people were killed in the earthquake, and the rest were terrified and gave glory to the God of heaven"* (Rev. 11:11–13).

How wonderful that the faithfulness of God never ceases, even if ours does; so, what will appear to be punishment will be actually intended by Him as a last instance effort to lead people on to salvation: *"Those whom I love, I reprove and discipline; therefore be zealous and repent"* (Rev. 3:19).

There is a fair amount of speculation among Bible scholars regarding the identity of the two witnesses. Some believe that Elijah will be one, for he did not experience death (2 Kings 2:9-11) and because it was prophesied that he would return in the later days: *"Behold, I am going to send you Elijah the prophet before the coming of the great and terrible day of the Lord"* (Mal. 4:5). Also, Elijah was given in the past the power to stop rain, as noted above.

Others believe that Moses will be one of the two witnesses, because although he died his body was buried by God (Deut. 34:6). He was also anointed to unleash the ten plagues on Egypt, and he was together with Elijah at the transfiguration of Christ (Matt. 17:3).

Lastly, others believe that Enoch will be one of the witnesses, because like Elijah, he was transferred to heaven without seeing death, and he was also a prophet of judgment like him.

Much have been written and discussed about their identity, which for some reason God chose not reveal to us. Some scholars feel, and the author agrees, that this is not a critical matter and should be left at that.

However, their mission and message are indeed to be highlighted for their great importance, that is, to call Israel to repentance at a time of great distress for them. Because of their stubbornness, *"all the nations of the earth will be gathered against it,"* though *"two parts in it will be cut off and perish; But the third* [the remnant] *will be left in it. And I will bring the third part through the fire, Refine them as silver is refined, And test them as gold is tested. They will call on My name, And I will answer them; I will say, 'They are my people,' And they will say, 'The Lord is my God'"* (Zech. 12:3; 13:8–9).

Babylon

The word *Babylon* originates from the ancient city of Bab-El (the "Gate of God"), which was founded by Nimrod, a descendant of Noah, who is mentioned in Genesis 10:8 as *"a mighty one on the earth."* However, he became a rebellious and arrogant king before God and forced his subjects *"to build...a city, and a tower whose top will reach into heaven."* But *God* confused *"'their language, so that they will not understand one another's speech.' So the Lord scattered them abroad from there over the whole earth"* (Gen. 11:4, 7–8). The tower's name was changed to Babel (which means "confusion"), and the project was abandoned.

Spiritual Babylon

Nimrod married Semiramis, identified as the first high-priestess of idolatry, who made Babylon "the mother of every heathen and pagan system in the world."[6] A satanic woman, she created the Babylonian mystery cult from which many ungodly rituals and practices originated and have filtered into various religions over the ages. She became the mother of Tammuz, who she claimed was miraculously conceived, while she publicly hailed him as the "promised deliverer," a false precursor of the Lord Jesus Christ. Semiramis portrayed herself, together with Tammuz, as a living representation of God, becoming a new world religion and ignoring the Word of God. This joint figure was later transferred to other religions, such as the Phoenician Astoreth and Tammuz, in Egypt as Isis and Horns, in Italy as Venus and Cupid, etc.

The prophet Ezekiel referred to these abominations in the harshest terms:

> Then He said to me, "Son of man, do you see what the elders of the house of Israel are committing in the dark, each man in the room of his carved images? For they say, 'The LORD does not see us; the LORD has forsaken the land." And He said to me, "Yet you will see greater abominations which they are committing." Then He brought me to the entrance of the gate to the Lord's house which was toward the north; and behold, women were sitting there weeping for Tammuz. And He said to me, "Do you see this, son of man? Yet you will see still greater abominations than these."
>
> —EZEKIEL 8:12–15

The sign of the cross was originally made sacred by Tammuz, because it represented the first letter of his name. This is why the sign of the cross can be found in a large number of ancient pagan altars and temples, and it did not originate with Christianity, as many believe, whose original symbol was the fish. Evidently, the sign of the cross later on acquired a completely different meaning and dimension for Christianity, after the crucifixion of the Lord Jesus Christ.

As these abominations and symbols of idolatry have existed over the centuries, the Lord refers to them in Revelation in very harsh terms:

> *Babylon the great was remembered before God, to give her the cup of the wine of His fierce wrath.*
>
> —REVELATION 16:19

> *Then one of the seven angels who had the seven bowls came and spoke with me, saying, "Come here, I will show you the judgment of the great harlot who sits on many waters [peoples, multitudes and nations], with whom the kings of the earth committed acts of immorality, and those who dwell on the earth were made drunk with the wine of her immorality." And he carried me away in the Spirit into a wilderness; and I saw a woman sitting on a scarlet beast, full of blasphemous names, having seven heads and ten horns. The woman was clothed in purple and scarlet, and adorned with gold and precious stones and pearls, having in her hand a gold cup full of abominations and of the unclean things of her immorality, and on her forehead a name was written, a mystery, "BABYLON THE GREAT, THE MOTHER OF HARLOTS AND OF THE ABOMINATIONS OF THE EARTH." And I saw the woman drunk with the blood of the saints, and with the blood of the witnesses of Jesus. When I saw her, I wondered greatly. And the angel said to me, "Why do you wonder? I will tell you the mystery of the woman and of the beast that carries her, which has the seven heads and the ten horns. The beast that you saw was, and is not [past], and is about to come up out of the abyss [the antichrist] and go to destruction. And those who dwell on the earth, whose name has not been written in the book of life from the foundation of the world, will wonder when they see the beast, that he was and is not and will come [the Antichrist, during the Tribulation]."*
> —REVELATION 17:1–8

The Antichrist will establish the base of his kingdom in Babylon, described in Revelation 17:9 as *"the seven *heads are seven mountains on which the woman sits,"* for which reason some have speculated that it will be Rome, the former head of the Roman Empire and the presumed capital of the antichrist's Federation of nations during the Tribulation, as noted earlier. Babylon, spiritually and materially, will become the source of abominations, idolatry, satanic rituals and practices represented in religious doctrines, images, and ceremonies loathsome to God.

Thus, God will put it in the heart of the Antichrist to destroy spiritual Babylon, as a competitive religious system, taking attention away from him. He will do so under the dispensation given to him by God to prevail over his opponents during the second half of the Tribulation period, as already discussed. Thus, he will use the ten-nation federation to destroy Babylon and its religious system.

> *And the ten horns which you saw, and the beast, these will hate the harlot and will make her desolate and naked, and will eat her flesh and will burn her up with fire. For God has put it their hearts to execute His purpose by having a common purpose, and by giving their kingdom to the beast, until the words of God should be fulfilled. And the woman whom you saw is the great city, which reigns over the kings of the earth.*
> —REVELATION 17:16–18

Political, Economic, and Commercial Babylon

As an extension of spiritual Babylon there will be a material city that will emerge as "the beauty of the kingdoms, the glory of the Chaldeans' pride" (Isa. 13:19). While historically this city was built and rebuilt over the centuries, its final destruction is prophesied in Revelation 18, as well as by Isaiah (Isa. 13–14) and Jeremiah (Jer. 50–51). This is targeted to occur in "the day of the Lord," in the latter part of the Tribulation period. According to some Bible commentators, there might be then a rebuilt Babylon (where it was originally located, at today's City of Hillah in the outskirts of Bagdad). Others believe that since its name symbolizes degradation and corruption, the prophecy could also apply to New York or London, presently the financial and commercial leading cities of the world.

After the destruction of spiritual Babylon at the hands of the Antichrist and material Babylon by the Antichrist's federation, John says:

> *I saw another angel coming down from heaven, having great authority, and the earth was illumined with his glory. And he cried out with a mighty voice, saying, "Fallen, fallen is Babylon the great! She has become a dwelling place of demons and a prison of every unclean spirit, and a prison of every unclean and hateful bird. For all the nations have drunk of the wine of the passion of her immorality, and the kings of the earth have committed acts of immorality with her, and the merchants of the earth have become rich by the wealth of her sensuality." I heard another voice from heaven, saying, "Come out of her, my people, so that you will not participate in her sins and receive of her plagues; for her sins have piled up as high as heaven, and God has remembered her iniquities."*
> —REVELATION 18:1–5

This strong, but at the same time merciful, warning from heaven is for men to remove themselves from today's Babylon, that is, from false religions; ungodly sects, organizations, and institutions; from evil wealth systems; economic plundering; greedy financial schemes; corruption; and immoral practices. Notice that a milder version of those prophesied evil practices are already going on at present involving a comparatively small circle of men and organizations yielding incredible power, manipulating virtual economies, currencies, gold, financing, banking, trade and commodities, as already discussed, while guided by evil forces toward the new world order.

> *And the kings of the earth, who committed acts of immorality and lived sensually with her, will weep and lament over her when they see the smoke of her burning, standing at a distance because of the fear of her torment, saying, "Woe, woe, the great city, Babylon, the strong city! For in one hour your judgment has come." And the merchants of the earth weep and mourn over her, because no one buys their cargoes any more.*
> —Revelation 18:9-11

How the mighty will fall in their iniquities in the day of reckoning! For in their selfishness and arrogance they will pursue richness and power without any concern for God, His Word, or His people. Even from a human point of view they will go beyond any legal, ethical, or moral boundaries. A lot of that is already going on at present, but in that day the end will be swift; in one hour its judgment will come.

Conversely, all godly and righteous people who will have been overwhelmed by those hoards of evildoers will raise their eyes to God and bless His name, for they will praise He who has brought justice and judgment to the world:

> "Rejoice over her, O heaven, and you saints and apostles and prophets, because God has pronounced judgment for you against her." Then a strong angel took up a stone like a great millstone and threw it into the sea, saying, "So will Babylon, the great city, be thrown down with violence, and will not be found any longer."
> —REVELATION 18:20–21

Thus, the destruction of worldly Babylon will be carried out by an angel of God while, paradoxically, the annihilation of spiritual Babylon will be executed by men under the leading of the Antichrist.

The Seven Trumpets

Revelation 8 and 9 depict the sounding of the seven trumpets. These no longer represent judgments but the execution of it with devastating power and reach:

- The *first* trumpet is to bring hail and fire, mixed with blood. A third of the earth, the trees, and the green grass will be burned up.

- The *second* will cast something like a great mountain burning with fire into the sea. A third of the sea will become blood, and a third of the sea creatures and the ships will be destroyed.

- The *third* will cause a great star from heaven burning like a torch to fall on a third of the rivers and springs of water, turning them to wormwood, and many men will die because of it.

- The *fourth* trumpet will sound, and a third of the sun, the moon, and the stars will be smitten, proportionally reducing their light.

- The *fifth* trumpet will cause a star to fall from heaven into the bottomless pit. The smoke going up from it like from a great furnace will darken the sun and the air. Out of the smoke will come forth locusts with the power of scorpions, but they will be told not to harm the grass, nor any green thing or trees, but only the men who do not have the seal of God on their foreheads.

- The *sixth* angel, at God's command, will release the four angels who are bound at the great river Euphrates, *"who had been prepared for the hour and day and month and year...so that they might kill a third of mankind. The number of the armies of the horsemen was two hundred million"* (Rev. 9:15–16). This is in reference to the war of Armageddon.

- The *seventh* angel sounded, *"and there were loud voices in heaven, saying, 'The kingdom of the world* [built by Satan through the Antichrist and the false prophet] *has become the kingdom of our Lord and of His Christ; and He will reign forever and ever"* (Rev. 11:15). This trumpet carries a word of encouragement instead of wrath, a message of reassurance for the Tribulation saints that God will prevail, a pause to build up their faith in Christ before the last outpouring of the wrath of God to follow.

The Seven Bowls

The true Christian church, the body of Christ, will no longer be on Earth during the Tribulation. The group who will be present includes most Jewish people and the survivors of Tribulation events, which will include the Tribulation saints, those who came to Christ and did not submit to the Antichrist after the church was raptured.

The release of the seven bowls (some translations addressed it as "vials"), which will occur in rapid succession, will be the most devastating series of events in world history. This will happen in the last portion of the Tribulation period, just before the second coming of the Lord.

While there is a certain parallelism with the plagues of Egypt recorded in Exodus 7 through 9, those were directed toward Pharaoh and his kingdom, whereas the bowls will fall on the whole Earth and have worldwide catastrophic consequences.

This is why the prophet Joel 2:31 calls it *"the great and awesome day of the Lord,"* and Malachi 4:5, *"the great and terrible day of the Lord."* There will be none like it.

The seven bowls of the wrath of God, poured by seven angels, are described in Revelation chapter 16. Although the first four replicate the chastisements addressed in the trumpet judgments and appear in the same order and number—pouring judgment upon the Earth, upon the sea, upon the rivers and fountains of water, and upon the

Sun—these judgments are not identified to be the same. Also, while the trumpet judgments will be poured upon all those inhabiting the earth at that time, the Scriptures make it clear that the first four bowls are targeted specifically at the Antichrist and his followers (those who received his mark) and to those who *"blasphemed the God of heaven because of their pains and their sores; and they did not repent of their deeds"* (Rev. 16:11).

- The first bowl: *"So the first angel went and poured out his bowl into the earth; and it became a loathsome and malignant sore upon the men who had the mark of the beast and who worshiped his image"* (Rev. 16:2).

- The second bowl: *"The second angel poured out his bowl into the sea; and it became blood like that of a dead man; and every living thing in the sea died"* (Rev. 16:3).

- The third bowl: *"Then the third angel poured out his bowl into the rivers and springs of waters; and they became blood"* (Rev. 16:4).

In order for us to understand the harshness of these judgments, the prophet John tells us what he heard from above:

> *The angel of the waters [was] saying: "Righteous are You, who are and who were, O Holy One, because You judged these things; for they poured out the blood of saints and prophets, and You have given them blood to drink. They deserve it." And I heard*

the altar saying, "Yes, O Lord God, the Almighty, true and righteous are Your judgments."
—REVELATION 16:5–7

Inasmuch as it is difficult for men to understand the extreme evilness, hatred, and arrogance of Satan, his angels, and his followers, it is no less difficult to comprehend the severity of God's judgments. But let it be restated that perfect justice demands condemnation for those that refuse perfect love, for those that decline His salvation, for those that reject the infinite grace of God freely offered to them through the sacrifice of Christ Jesus at the cross. As the apostle Paul said, *"Behold then the kindness and severity of God; to those who fell, severity, but to you, God's kindness, if you continue in His kindness"* (Rom. 11:22).

- The fourth bowl: *"The fourth angel poured out his bowl upon the sun, and it was given to it to scorch men with fire. Men were scorched with fierce heat; and they blasphemed the name of God who has the power over these plagues, and they did not repent so as to give Him glory"* (Rev. 16:8–9).

- The fifth bowl: *"Then the fifth angel poured out his bowl upon the throne of the beast, and his kingdom became darkened; and they gnawed their tongues because of pain, and they blasphemed the God of heaven because of their pains and their sores; and they did not repent of their deeds"* (Rev. 16:10–11).

- The sixth bowl: *"The sixth angel poured out his bowel upon the great river, the Euphrates; and its water was dried up, so that the way would be prepared for the kings from the east. And I saw coming out of the mouth of the dragon and out of the mouth of the beast and out of the mouth of the false prophet, three unclean spirits like frogs; for they are spirits of demons, performing signs, which go out to the* kings of the whole world, to gather them together for the war of the great day of God, the Almighty. *('Behold, I am coming like a thief. Blessed is the one who stays awake and keeps his clothes, so that he will not walk about naked and men will not see his shame.') And they gathered them together to the place which in Hebrew is called Har-Magedon"* (Rev. 16:12–16, emphasis added).

It is important to clarify a few things about this scripture. Notice that *all nations* will gather together to fight against Israel (Rev. 16:14). Such a unified and unprecedented position amongst the peoples of the world will be the consequence of a number of factors:

- They do not know, or have not believed in the Word of God, and neither have they realized that the apparent prevalence of evil will be only temporary to test the dwellers of the Earth. Further, they do not know that it will occur solely because of the dispensation granted by God to Satan, the Antichrist, and the false prophet during the last phase of the Tribulation period.

- The degree of deception that will be created by the Antichrist (energized by Satan) and the false prophet will be great, as their satanic doctrines will be supported with great signs and wonders.

- Most world leaders will be prompted to turn against God because they will be convinced that the Antichrist will prevail over the Lord. For others, their hate for God will be prompted by their inability to deal with the catastrophic events poured out on the nations via the trumpet and bowl judgments. Thus, going after Israel will become the only presumably viable or ostensible way to "get back at God" and, in their colossal madness, to attempt to subdue Him.

- The Holy Spirit and His arm, the church, will not be on earth to restrain the forces of evil, nor to shed light on this massive deception, which could even involve the broad use of submissive drugs. Tests of this kind of drugs intended for massive use are being conducted today as a milder version of other lethal forms of biological warfare, as was recently evidenced in the Syrian civil war. The words pestilence and plagues used in various end-time Bible prophecies can be clearly associated with biological weapons.

Armageddon will be a war (not a battle) comprising several confrontations to be fought against Israel during the latter part of the Tribulation period, as will be discussed later in this chapter. It will be fought at a place named "Har," for "mountain," and "Megiddo," named for an ancient city north of Israel that was on a hill overlooking several valleys (the Jezreel, Esdraelon, and Taanach) and the plains of Megiddo, where the armies of the world will gather to confront Israel and their God, who will utterly destroy them. In centuries past, many battles were fought by Israel in that area (approximately two hundred square miles), and so have the armies from many nations since the days of Nebuchadnezzar, king of Assyria. The prophet Joel refers to Armageddon, as follows: *"For behold, in those days and at that time, When I restore the fortunes of Judah and Jerusalem, I will gather all the nations And bring them down to the valley of Jehoshaphat [representing the above named valleys and plains]. Then I will enter into judgment with them there On behalf of My people and My inheritance, Israel"* (Joel 3:1–2).

- *The seventh bowl: "Then the seventh angel poured out his bowl upon the air, and a loud voice came out of the temple from the throne, saying, "It is done." And there were flashes of lightning and sounds and peals of thunder; and there was a great earthquake, such as there had not been since man came to be upon the earth, so great an earthquake was it, and so mighty. The great city was split into three parts, and the cities of the nations fell. Babylon the great was remembered before God, to give her the cup of the wine of His fierce wrath. And every island fled away, and the mountains were not found. And huge hailstones, about one hundred pounds each, came down from heaven upon men; and men blasphemed God because of the plague of the hail, because its plague was extremely severe"* (Rev. 16:17–21).

THE WAR OF ARMAGEDDON

As commented above, Armageddon is going to be a war involving several battles that will take place during the Tribulation period. The great, final confrontation will incorporate all nations and will be fought openly at Har-Megiddo against Israel and the Lord Himself. This war will culminate with the second coming of the Lord Jesus Christ with His heavenly armies, the total destruction of ungodly forces, and the throwing of the Antichrist and the false prophet *"alive into the lake of fire which burns with brimstone"* (Rev. 19:20). Satan will be bound and locked *"into the abyss"* for *"a thousand years"* (Rev. 20:2–3).

It must be noted that the war of Armageddon will take place after the seal judgments have been executed through the outpouring of trumpets and bowls, resulting in catastrophic world conditions. More than half of the world population will be killed, along with an equal share of vegetation and ocean life destroyed by fire and brimstone, while fresh water will become undrinkable.

This war will commence with the northern invasion of Israel, addressed above, instigated by the Antichrist and led by Russia and its allies (Germany, Turkey, Persia, Libya, Ethiopia, and Egypt) in pursuit of great spoil. However, these strong invading forces will be decimated by the direct intervention of the Lord through natural disasters aimed at them (a great earthquake, torrential rain, hailstone, fire and brimstone) and by causing conflict in which *"every man's sword will be against his brother"* (Ezek. 38:21-22).

The Battle of Armageddon is not to be confused with the northern invasion previously addressed in this book. The later, northern invasion is to be fought by Russia and its allies from the north against Israel. It will be led by Gog, it will take place during the first half of the Tribulation period, and it will generate the protest of some nations because the objective is a great spoil. The Lord will utterly defeat them via great natural convulsions, pestilence, and confusion. Conversely, the final battle of Armageddon will involve all the nations of the world, it will be led by the Antichrist against Israel and God, it will take place at the end of the Tribulation period and cause no protests, and it will end with the total destruction of ungodly forces at the mountains of Israel (Ezek. 39:2-4). Defeat will come about by the word of Christ:

> *And I saw heaven opened, and behold, a white horse, and He who sat on it is called Faithful and True, and in righteousness He judges and wages war. His eyes are a flame of fire, and on His head are many diadems; and He has a name written on Him which no one knows except Himself. He is clothed with a robe dipped in blood, and His name is called The Word of God. And the armies which are in heaven, clothed in fine linen, white and clean, were following Him on white horses. From His mouth comes a sharp sword, so that with it He may strike down the nations, and He will rule them with a rod of iron; and He treads the wine press of the fierce wrath of God, the Almighty. And on His robe and on His*

thigh He has a name written, "KING OF KINGS, AND LORD OF LORDS."
—REVELATION 19:11–16

In between these preliminary battles, prior to the final confrontation, there will be other movements of troops, such as the ones from the kings of the east (presumably the modern nations of India, Pakistan, China, Russia, and Japan, all east of Israel), for which purpose the Lord will cause the Euphrates River to dry up in order to allow the passage of a-200-million-man army toward Armageddon (Rev. 9:16; 16:12).

Other participants will include the king of the south, a North African power or group of nations; and the Roman federation, the former Roman Empire, where the throne of the Antichrist will be. Other current countries and continents are not mentioned in the Bible for obvious reasons, but the Scriptures do assert, *"Indeed, My decision is to gather nations, To assemble kingdoms, To pour out on them My indignation; All my burning anger; For all the earth will be devoured By the fire of My zeal"* (Zeph. 3:8).

The horrendous carnage and destruction from the defeat of all the evil armies of the world caused John to behold *"an angel standing in the sun, and he cried out with a loud voice, saying to all the birds which fly in midheaven, 'Come, assemble for the great supper of God, so that you may eat the flesh of the kings and the flesh of the commanders and the flesh of mighty men and the flesh of horses and of those who sit on them and the flesh of all men, both free men and slaves, and small and great'"* (Rev. 19:18). This will represent the physical and spiritual cleansing of the earth before the establishment of the one-thousand-year kingdom of Christ on Earth (Rev. 20:6).

Who will physically survive Armageddon? The remnant of Israel at Petra (Zech. 13:8–9) and the Tribulation saints whose lives were spared from martyrdom.

Who will spiritually survive this test? The Word says:

> *Then I saw thrones, and they sat on them, and judgment was given to them. And I saw the souls of those who had been beheaded because of their testimony of Jesus and because of the word of God, and those who had not worshiped the beast or his image, and had not received the mark on their forehead and on their hand; and they came to life and reigned with Christ for a thousand years. The rest of the dead did not come to life until the thousand years were completed. This is the first resurrection. Blessed and holy is the one who has a part in the first resurrection; over these the second death has no power, but they will be priests of God and of Christ and will reign with Him for a thousand years.*
> —REVELATION 20:4–6

THE SECOND COMING

It is important to refresh in our memory that the Lord Jesus Christ is the Word and that, as He told the "religious" Jews concerning the Scriptures, *"It is these that testify about Me"* (John 5:39).

Thirty-seven explicit and direct prophesies were fulfilled in His first coming, quoted and referred to in the first chapter of this book as irrefutable evidence of the accuracy and veracity of the Word of God. He originally came as a humble and meek servant, not to judge but to serve and save whosoever would believe in Him, as He is the way, the truth, and life. While *"the world was made through Him, and the world did not know Him. He came* to His own, and those that were His own did not receive Him. But as many as received Him, to them He gave the right to become children of God, even to those who believed in His name" (John 1:10–12). He did not regard equality with God as a thing to be grasped, *"but emptied Himself, taking the form of a bond-servant, and being made in the likeness of men. Being found in appearance as a man, He humbled Himself by becoming obedient to the point of death, even death on a cross"* (Phil. 2:6–8). He was mocked and despised, yet He forgave and prayed for those who crucified Him. His death and resurrection two thousand years ago ushered in the greatest outpouring of love the world has ever known, but now the time of judgment— *"the great and awesome day of the Lord"* (Joel 2:31)—is at hand.

The second coming of the Lord Jesus Christ should occur as no surprise to anyone acquainted with the Bible, least of all to Jews and Christians. The second advent of the Messiah is specifically referred to one thousand eight hundred and forty-five times in the Scriptures (one thousand five hundred and twenty-seven times in the Old Testament and three hundred and eighteen times in the New Testament). This time His advent will be very different from the first one:

While He will *"come in just the same way as you have watched Him go into heaven"* (Acts 1:11), it will be in His resurrected body, and His infinite majesty will be manifest and visible to all:

> *The sun will be darkened, and the moon will not give its light, and the stars will fall from the sky, and the powers of the heavens will be shaken. And then the sign of the Son of Man will appear in the sky, and*

then the tribes of the earth will mourn, and they will see the Son of Man coming on the clouds of the sky with power and great glory.
—MATTHEW 24:29–30

To those that mocked, despised, and rejected Him, the fear of a judgment infinitely more severe than death will take a hold of them. The Word denotes, *"But the day of the Lord will come like a thief, in which the heavens will pass away with a roar and the elements will be destroyed with intense heat, and the earth and its works will be burned up"* (2 Pet. 3:10). The Lord will come with His saints and with *"the armies which are in heaven…From His mouth comes a sharp sword, so that with it He may strike down the nations"* (Rev. 19:14–15).

There are Bible interpreters who endeavor to provide a nonliteral or "spiritualized" view as to how and through whom Jesus will attain His victory. However, the Word is vividly clear as to how the wrath of the Lord will manifest itself at the final battle:

Now this will be the plague with which the Lord will strike all the peoples who have gone to war against Jerusalem; their flesh will rot while they stand on their feet, and their eyes will rot in their sockets, and their tongue will rot in their mouth. It will come about in that day that a great panic from the Lord will fall on them; and they will seize one another's hand, and the hand of one will be lifted against the hand of another.
—ZECHARIAH 14:12–13

Thus, those who lack faith and humanize their understanding of the Almighty are unable to comprehend

God's infinite power and determination. Our Christ, who called the universe and everything that was created into existence, needs no help from anyone. With the sole expression of His will, which is the will of the Father, it will come to pass. If He calls us to join Him or to do His will, it is simply because He delights to make those who love Him and believe in Him participants of His works and of His glory.

The understanding of His Word requires prayer, always prayer, seeking the revelation of the Holy Spirit, for as noted earlier in this book, *"we also speak, not in words taught by human wisdom, but in those taught by the Spirit, combining spiritual thoughts with spiritual words"* (1 Cor. 2:13).

The Lord will return to the very place from which He departed: *"In that day His feet will stand on the Mount of Olives, which is in front of Jerusalem on the east; and the Mount of Olives will be split in its middle from east to west by a very large valley, so that half of the mountain will move toward the north and the other half toward the south"* (Zech. 14:4).

The second coming of the Lord will not be seen just by a host of angels and a few humble shepherds, as in His first advent, but *"every eye will see Him, even those who pierced Him; and all the tribes of the earth will mourn over Him"* (Rev. 1:7).

Christ's coming will bring about the first resurrection, involving all those who died in Christ, who did not worship the Beast nor receive his mark, as previously noted (Rev. 20:1–6).

The Millennium

The word *millennium* originates from the Latin *mille* ("one thousand") and *annum* ("years"). Others trace its origin to the word *chiliasm* (from *chilioi*, meaning "one thousand"). This term relates to a large number of biblical prophesies in the Old and the New Testament that specifically address two types of restorations, a spiritual restoration and the restoration of the Earth and of Heaven.

A spiritual restoration—with the establishment of the kingdom of Jesus Christ on Earth, along with the risen saints as priests of God for a thousand years—will happen immediately after His second coming, at the end of the Tribulation period, when He will utterly destroy the forces of evil from all nations at Armageddon and throw the Beast and the false prophet into the lake of fire. Satan, on the other hand, will be bound for a thousand years:

> *Then I saw an angel coming down from heaven, holding the key of the abyss and a great chain in his hand. And he laid hold of the dragon, the serpent of old, who is the devil and Satan, and bound him for a thousand years; and he threw him into the abyss, and shut it and sealed it over him, so that he would not deceive the nations any longer, until the thousand years were completed; after these things he must be released for a short time.*
> —Revelation 20:1–3

A restoration of the Earth and Heaven will take place after the horrendous devastation brought about by the wrath of God and the resulting judgments, as noted. However, the promises of God do not go unfulfilled, as written in Isaiah 65:17–19: *"For behold, I create new heavens and a new earth; And the former things shall not be remembered or come to mind. But be glad and rejoice forever in what I create; For behold, I create Jerusalem for rejoicing, And her people for gladness. I will also rejoice in Jerusalem, and be glad in My people; And there will no longer be heard in her The voice of weeping and the sound of crying."*

A few other scriptures from the Old Testament, of many, involving promises made to the Jewish people about the kingdom of God on Earth have been selected herein to illustrate its significance for a community that through history has been devoid of peace:

> *And He will strike the earth with the rod of His mouth, And with the breath of His lips He will slay the wicked. Also righteousness will be the belt about His loins, And faithfulness the belt about His waist. And the wolf will dwell with the lamb, And the leopard will lie down with the young goat, And the calf and the young lion and the fatling together; And a little boy will lead them. Also the cow and the bear will graze, Their young will lie down together, And the lion will eat straw like the ox. The nursing child will play by the hole of the cobra, And the weaned child will put his hand on the viper's den. They will not hurt or destroy in all My holy mountain, For the earth will be full of the knowledge of the Lord As the waters cover the sea.*
> —Isaiah 11:4–9

The curse of God upon the earth brought about by sin at the Garden of Eden will be removed, and the peace of Christ will reign for one thousand years, with Satan bound in the abyss, until all traces of evil are cleansed.

> They will see the glory of the Lord, The majesty of our God. Encourage the exhausted, and strengthen the feeble. Say to those with anxious heart, "Take courage, fear not. Behold, your God will come with vengeance; The recompense of God will come, But He will save you." Then the eyes of the blind will be opened And the ears of the deaf will be unstopped. Then the lame will leap like a deer, And the tongue of the mute will shout for joy. For waters will break forth in the wilderness And streams in the Arabah. The scorched land will become a pool And the thirsty ground springs of water; In the haunt of jackals, its resting place, Grass becomes reeds and rushes. A highway will be there, a roadway, And it will be called the Highway of Holiness. The unclean will not travel on it, But it will be for him who walks that way, And fools will not wander on it. No lion will be there, Nor will any vicious beast go up on it; These will not be found there. But the redeemed will walk there, And the ransomed of the Lord will return And come with joyful shouting to Zion, With everlasting joy upon their heads. They will find gladness and joy, And sorrow and sighing will flee away.
> —Isaiah 35:2–10

Human illnesses and physical maladies, thirst and scorched land will be no more, and sorrow will be replaced by gladness and joy.

> "Behold, the days are coming," declares the Lord, "When I will raise up for David a righteous Branch; And He will reign as king and act wisely And do justice and righteousness in the land. "In His days Judah will be saved, And Israel will dwell securely;

> And this is His name by which He will be called, 'The Lord our righteousness.'"
>
> —JEREMIAH 23:5–6

This is a beautiful promise from God about Christ's kingdom on Earth, where justice and righteousness will prevail. And there will be safety in the land.

> Then you will know that I am the Lord your God, Dwelling in Zion, My holy mountain. So Jerusalem will be holy, And strangers will pass through it no more.
>
> —JOEL 3:17

In Jerusalem will rest the throne of Christ.

> And the Lord will be king over all the earth; in that day the Lord will be the only one, and His name the only one.... People will live in it, and there will no longer be a curse, for Jerusalem will dwell in security.
>
> —ZECHARIAH 14:9, 11

The promise is safety and peace are long-desired conditions for all, but especially for the Jewish people, and it will come to pass.

In the New Testament there are a number of scriptures concordant with the above Old Testament ones:

> I say to you that many will come from the east and west, and recline at table with Abraham, Isaac, and Jacob in the kingdom of heaven.
>
> —MATTHEW 8:11

So the promise is for the remnant of Judah and Israel, and for the Lord's church and the Tribulation saints.

> *The time is fulfilled, and the kingdom of God is at hand; repent and believe in the gospel.*
>
> —MARK 1:15

This call is for whoever receives this message: Jews and Gentiles. *Heed His word while there is still time.*

> *And that He may send Jesus, the Christ appointed for you, whom heaven must receive until the period of restoration of all things about which God spoke by the mouth of His holy prophets from ancient time.*
>
> —ACTS 3:20–21

So, Christ is now in heaven at the right hand of the Father. After His second coming He will establish His millennium kingdom, the period of restoration of all things prior to eternity. This will take place, first, through spiritual blessings that were lost by the nations when they turned their back on Christ's salvation, and second, by the physical restoration of an earth cursed by God because of man's rebellion.

> *Blessed and holy is the one who has a part in the first resurrection; over these the second death has no power, but they will be priests of God and of Christ and will reign with Him for a thousand years.*
>
> —REVELATION 20:6

This is also addressed in John 5:28–29:

> *Do not marvel at this: for an hour is coming, in which all who are in the tombs will hear His voice, and will come forth; those who did good deeds to a resurrection of life [the first resurrection], those*

who committed the evil deeds to a resurrection of judgment [the second resurrection].

The latter will not occur until the Millennium has lapsed:

And the rest of the dead did not come to life until the thousand years were completed.
—REVELATION 20:5

Who will remain on Earth during the Millennium period? The remnant of Israel and the earthly saints who survived the Tribulation, and their descendants. These will repopulate the Earth under conditions similar to those intended by God for Adam and Eve and their descendants, and for Noah and his family after the Flood. But in the case of the Millennium, the infinite difference will be that the Lord Jesus Christ will be on Earth ruling and reigning from Jerusalem and that Satan will be shut and sealed in the abyss, no longer being able to deceive the nations until the one thousand years elapse. On the other hand, the resurrected saints, in their incorruptible bodies, will be priests and reign along with Him for a thousand years. It will be a perfect kingdom, full of the grace of God, ruled with righteousness; exempted of wars; full of peace, joy, and economic prosperity, where people will live longer and free of deceases with direct access to the perfect Physician. Like in any healthy earthly community, surely there will be works and tasks to perform. For the human inhabitants, there will be both spiritual and community works (Isa. 65). For the resurrected saints, they will serve as priests and governors of Christ, ministering to the saints (*"You were faithful with a few things, I will put you in charge of many things"* [Matt. 25:21]).

In the light of such a magnificent kingdom, with the Lord at the helm, God's dispensation to allow the reappearance of Satan is disconcerting to many people today, and surely it will be equally so to those at the end of the Millennium:

> *When the thousand years are completed, Satan will be released from his prison, and will come out to deceive the nations which are in the four corners of the earth, Gog and Magog, to gather them together for the war; the number of them is like the sand of the seashore. And they came up on the broad plain of the earth and surrounded the camp of the saints and the beloved city, and fire came down from heaven and devoured them. And the devil who deceived them was thrown into the lake of fire and brimstone, where the beast and the false prophet are also; and they will be tormented day and night forever and ever.*
> —REVELATION 20:7–10

Some comments about this important scripture appear in order:

1. The central message is that Satan will receive a short-term dispensation from God to *"come out to deceive the nations which are in the four corners of the earth, Gog and Magog, to gather them together for the war."* It is clear, therefore, that this resurgence of evil will again involve all nations, including the future end-time leader of Russia (Gog and Magog). While he is similar in name to he who will lead one thousand years earlier

the northern invasion of Israel at the outset of the war of Armageddon (as addressed above), obviously he will be a different leader than the one who will be killed in the earlier conflict (Ezek. 39:4).

2. Again, Satan's final deception will prompt the gathering of a large army to attack the camp of the saints and Jerusalem, where the very throne of Christ on Earth will be. But this time the Lord will deal swiftly with this revolt with fire from heaven. Satan will be thrown into the lake of fire and brimstone to join the Beast and the false prophet into eternal torment. This prophetic judgment and the eternal and final eradication of evil will then take place.

3. To the author of this book, the outcome of Satan's direct struggle against God was an obvious and foregone conclusion. But it is simply bewildering that a large number of Millennium men could again be tempted to rebel against the kingdom of Jesus Christ on Earth while enjoying His glory and all the marvelous blessings and benefits of His realm. How will they be induced to such a disconcerting level of madness and insanity? How will they be so blind? Some biblical and historical antecedents might help us understand such irrational and irreverent behavior and provide a very serious lesson for us today:

- Satan's deceptiveness cannot be underestimated. It worked for him with Adam and Eve, and the whole world was cursed and suffered over thousands of years for it.

- It happened to the people of Judah and Israel throughout history, and the Old Testament provides ample evidence of that. Their history shows a never ending succession of periods of blessings from the Lord followed by His people's rejection, ingratitude, and sin, only to cause them to suffer punishment, captivity, and devastation as corrective measures from God.

- It happened after Jesus' ascent to Heaven and the martyrdom of the initial Christian church took place. This admonishment and example was ignored by many who subsequently introduced political power, wealth, and immorality into the church while denying access to the Word to the social outcasts, to the poor, and the illiterate. The consequences over the centuries were continuous wars, pestilence, and famine—God's punishment for spiritual negligence and apostasy.

- It happens today to nominal Christians and most other religious people who maintain an outward appearance of godliness but in their hearts are evil. The Lord Jesus called them hypocrites, fools, blind men, serpents, a brood of vipers, and whitewashed tombs. He warned them, *"How shall you escape the sentence of hell?"* (Matt. 23:33).

Thus, when the Millennium is looked at from the above-noted historical perspective, one can somewhat comprehend that the fundamental problem will continue to lie in the unstable, ungrateful, unfaithful, and inherently wicked nature of men: *"The heart is more deceitful than all else And is desperately sick; Who can understand it?"* (Jer. 17:9). This will reaffirm the fallen nature of man and that their only way to the truth and life is through faith in the Lord Jesus Christ, in the loving reassurance of His redeeming sacrifice at the cross, and in their sincere repentance and desire to conform to His will.

The Lord said, *"For apart from Me you can do nothing"* (John 15:5), while conversely, the apostle Paul emphatically declared, *"I can do all things through Him who strengthens me"* (Phil. 4:13). Thus, the Millennium will become the ultimate test for men, at the end of which period there will be no further excuses or explanations, nor a chance for repentance. Men, in the use of their God-given free will and at the height of God's blessings, will have to opt to follow Christ's will or their own. The fullness and magnificent reality of the Lord Jesus Christ will be before their eyes in Jerusalem providing spiritual guidance, justice, order, and blessings of every nature to everyone in His kingdom. No longer will the existence or nature of God be in doubt, nor the veracity of His promises and blessings. Therefore, the period for God's salvation will be then closed for eternity.

Thus, on what will Satan base a convincing argument in order to tempt so many Millennium saints to go into war?

The reader must understand that as wars will have been eradicated during the Millennium, Satan's proposed revolt will be directly against the Lord Jesus Christ's authority. Whereas the Word does not say on what enticing argument Satan will base his deception, one may speculate from past experiences, as follows.

Pride

Pride was the cause of Satan's own fall. He was a cherubim who inhabited the very presence of God, and yet he rebelled against Him, longing to be like Him. Shockingly, one-third of the angels of heaven followed Satan, only to be defeated by the archangel Michael and his angels. Satan and his fallen angels were subsequently cast down to Earth and ultimately into the lake of fire, as addressed earlier in this book.

Pride, that selfish and distorted feeling directly opposite to the prime commandment to love God above all things, and our fellow men like ourselves, will also be present in men during the Millennium and could become the main cause of Satan's temptation. After all, Satan even tried to tempt Jesus Christ Himself after He fasted forty days in the dessert, offering Him the kingdoms of this world!

Man's Flesh Is Weak

Man's flesh is indeed weak, and Millennium men will continue to be exposed to the temptations of the flesh, which, as you know, are opposite to the Spirit. The fact that men will enjoy perfect health and blessings of all kinds during the Millennium will not preclude them from being tempted to pursue things beyond those allowed by God. Our own experience frequently proves that we get closer to God in times of difficulty, while we become negligent and aloof in periods of prosperity.

Satan's Revolt

His revolt will be brief and his defeat conclusive, *"for fire [will come] down from heaven and devoured them"* (Rev. 20:9). Satan will join the Beast and the false prophet, along with all those who followed them, into eternal damnation. That will be the end of evil.

Other Interpretations

The author does not wish to close the Millennium chapter without making a brief comparative reference of the pre-Millennial doctrine with other interpretations regarding this important subject.

The Pre-Millennial Doctrine

As previously noted, the pre-Millennial doctrine is the biblical interpretation endorsed by the author of this book under the guidance of the Holy Spirit and the scriptural support amply exposed to you. Readers have been able to review and discern Bible texts that extensively address the nature, timing, and purpose of the prophecies that support the pre-Millennial doctrine. These truths were upheld by the apostles and the early church (through the year A.D. 300) and affirm that the second coming of the Lord Jesus Christ will occur at the end of the Tribulation period, prior to the establishment of His millennium kingdom on Earth. At that time He will return to Earth with great glory and power, along with His saints and angelic host, to utterly defeat the armies of the nations led by the Antichrist and the false prophet at Armageddon and to throw them down into the lake of fire.

The underlying premise of this doctrine is *the literal interpretation of the Word of God*, as it is written. It further advocates that scriptures must be carefully and extensively reviewed via concordances and historical references to ascertain their meaning and significance. Christ Himself was very explicit about it when He said, *"Do not think that I came to abolish the Law or the Prophets; I did not come to abolish but to fulfill. For truly I say to you, until heaven and earth pass away, not the smallest letter or stroke shall pass from the Law until all is accomplished"* (Matt. 5:17-18). Moreover, the Book of Revelation has one of the most severe warnings from the Lord to those who either add or take away from His Word: *"I testify to everyone who hears the words of the prophecy of this book: if anyone adds to them, God will add to him the plagues which are written in this book; if anyone takes away from the words of the book of this prophecy, God will take away his part from the tree of life and from the holy city, which are written in this book. He who testifies to these things says, 'Yes, I am coming quickly.' Amen, Come, Lord Jesus"* (Rev. 22:18-20).

The Amillennial Doctrine

The main exponent of the amillennial interpretation was St. Augustine (A.D. 354-430), a philosopher and theologian who significantly influenced western eschatology in the Middle Ages and even some of the later Reformers of the church (e.g., Luther and Calvin). He wrote three widely read books at the time, *On Christian Doctrine*, *The City of God*, and *Confessions*, which gain for him the recognition of one of the thirty-three doctors of the Catholic church. In his early days, however, he was a pre-Millennialist but later on converted to amillennialism as a reaction against Donatists (pre-Millennial "liberals"), who, based on the prophesied millennial kingdom of Christ on Earth, promoted a certain degree of earthly permissiveness in Christian life, such as excessive use of food, wine, and jovial celebrations. That sect also introduced allegorical interpretations of the Word of God, an approach that would later on end up actually influencing Augustine himself.

In fact, Augustine's main doctrinal departure from the early church, and with pre-Millennialism, was based on his "spiritualized" view of biblical interpretation rather than on an adherence to what scriptural texts actually say. This was so contrary to the position conveyed by him in his book *Arguments on the Existence of God*, Chapter 10, "How to Discern Whether a Phrase Is Figurative," paragraph fourteen, where he warns that "we must also pay heed to that which tells us not to take a literal form of speech as if it were figurative."

Examples of these "spiritualized" interpretations included Augustine's belief that the millennium kingdom of Christ on Earth referred only to the spiritual realm and not to an earthly or tangible kingdom. Thus, he did not believe that an actual Millennium kingdom of Christ on Earth will exist. Further, to justify his optimism that the church would continue to grow and prosper spiritually in the future, Augustine vouched that Satan was in fact bound to the Abyss upon Jesus Christ's *first* coming, not after His second coming, as Scriptures assert. Therefore, he explained, the church will continue to prosper until His second coming, when judgment will take place. The author of this book has already provided clear and multiple scriptures that deny those interpretations, while spiritual, moral, and social reality since Augustine's time makes it evident that Satan is anything but bound and remains as malignantly active as ever after Christ's first coming: *"Children, it is the last hour; and just as you have heard that antichrist is coming, even now many antichrists have arisen; from this we know that it is the last hour"* (1 John 2:18).

This amillennial position also ignores the explicit Tribulation signs and warnings, as well as its judgments upon the Earth (the seals, the trumpets, and the bowls), as explicitly addressed in Revelation. (They believe in a symbolic Tribulation instead.)

Moreover, Augustine refused to acknowledge Revelation 20, which describes a "millennial kingdom on Earth" (the "theocratic kingdom"), because he contended that the Word says that the kingdom of Christ will last forever and not just one thousand years. Whereas we most definitely agree that Christ will reign forever, what Augustine failed to recognize was the prophetic pronouncement of the apostle Paul, when he asserted:

> *Then comes the end, when He hands over the kingdom to the God and Father, when He has abolished all rule and all authority and power. For He must reign until He has put all His [the Father's] enemies under His feet. The last enemy that will be abolished is death. For He [the Father] has put all things in subjection under His feet [the Son]. But when He says, "All things are put in subjection," it is evident that He [the Father] is excepted who put all things in subjection to Him [the Son]. When all things are subjected to Him, then the Son Himself also will be subjected to the One who subjected all things to Him,* that God may be all in all.
>
> —1 CORINTHIANS 15:24–28, EMPHASIS ADDED

This scripture will be explained further later when we discuss the end of the millennial kingdom and its merger into the eternal kingdom of God, where in unity the Father, the Son, and the Holy Spirit will reign forever.

Postmillennialism

Postmillennialism is similar to amillennialism, but they believe that there will be an actual Tribulation period before the second coming of the Lord, after which He will conduct the Last Judgment.

Merger of the Millennium Kingdom with the Eternal Kingdom of God

As noted, at the end of the Millennium and after the brief release of Satan from the abyss, he will pursue his final rebellion along with the betraying saints that follow him. This attempt against the theocracy of God and the reigning Christ will be utterly defeated. This event will close forever the battle between good and evil both on Earth and in Heaven.

Thereafter, Jesus Christ, to whom all things will then have been finally subjected by the Father, will in turn subject His earthly kingdom to the Father so that there may be one kingdom of God for ever and ever under one God, *"That God may be all in all"* (1 Cor. 15:28) through eternity. Amen.

The Great White Throne

The Great White Throne represents the judgment seat of Jesus Christ, from which He will administer final justice to those that rebelled or denied Him. This will be a judgment of eternal damnation for all those whose names are not written in the Book of Life. Revelation 20:11–15 reads:

> *Then I saw a great white throne and Him who sat upon it, from whose presence earth and heaven fled away, and no place was found for them. And I saw the dead, the great and the small, standing before the throne, and books were opened; and another book was opened, which is the book of life; and the dead were judged from the things which were written in the books, according to their deeds. And the sea gave up the dead which were in it, and death and Hades gave up the dead which were in them; and they were judged, every one of them according to their deeds. Then death and Hades were thrown into the lake of fire. This is the second death, the lake of fire. And if anyone's name was not found written in the book of life, he was thrown into the lake of fire.*

It should be noted that judgment pertains to Christ: *"For not even the Father judges any one, but He has given all judgment to the Son, so that all will honor the Son even as they honor the Father"* (John 5:22-23).

The magnitude of an offense is determined by who the offender is and by who he has offended. When men sin, that means that they have chosen to separate themselves from God in the exercise of their free will rather than to do God's will. While God has given men freedom to choose, He has also given them a testimony of His glory (Ps. 19:1, *"The heavens are telling of the glory of God"*) and of His love (1 Thess. 5:9-10, *"For God has not destined us for wrath, but for obtaining salvation through our Lord Jesus Christ, who died for us"*) and of His will (the Word of God). For this reason, men *"are without excuse"* (Rom. 1:20).

To the readers of this book, take notice: while the

kingdom of God is at hand, *"draw near God and He will draw near you"* (James 4:8).

The Creation of a New Heaven and a New Earth

There are various interpretations amongst Bible scholars about the promise in the Word of a new Heaven and a new Earth. While there is no question about the promise itself, especially after the devastation suffered by Earth during the Tribulation period, the issue revolves around which scriptures actually refer to the millennial kingdom and which ones to the eternal kingdom of God.

It appears clear that Old Testament scriptures on the subject refer to the millennial kingdom and do not go beyond that, as prophesied by Isaiah 65, wherein the existence of death, earthly tasks, and the bearing of children during the Millennium are mentioned; and Isaiah 66, where *"the corpses of the men Who have transgressed against Me"* (v. 24) were still visible as a witness—all of which will not exist or be remembered in the eternal kingdom of God.

In the New Testament, however, in Revelation 21, *"a new heaven and a new earth"* (v. 1) is presented in a different manner, and it does not appear to relate to the millennial kingdom on Earth:

- *"For the first heaven and the first earth passed away, and there is no longer any sea"* (Rev. 21:1): This is a different notion to the restoration to take place during the Millennium.

- *"And I saw the holy city, new Jerusalem, coming down out of heaven from God"* (v. 2): From the thorough description in verses 9 through 25 it obviously does not refer to the Millennial Jerusalem on Earth.

- *"And there will no longer be any death...the first things have passed away"* (v. 4): This contrasts the Millennium, when death will still exist.

- *"And He who sits on the throne said, 'Behold, I am making all things new"* (v. 5): This affirmation could not be made about the Millennium's restoration

- *"And He said to me: 'It is done. I am the Alpha and the Omega, the beginning and the end. I will give the one who thirsts from the spring of the water of life without cost'"* (v. 6): There is no reference to this in the Millennium scriptures, where food and water are alluded to.

- *"I saw no temple in it, for the Lord God the Almighty and the Lamb are its temple"* (v. 22): Conversely, there will be a temple during the Millennium.

- *"And the city has no need of the sun or of the moon to shine on it, for the glory of God has illuminated it, and its lamp is the Lamb"* (v. 23): There is no indication about this in the Millennium period.

The above scriptures seem to point out certain aspects of the eternal kingdom of God, notwithstanding that a few references in Revelation 21 are interpreted by some to be Millennial in context. Consider, for example, verse 9: *"One of the seven angels who had the seven bowls,"* which could be just a way to identify him, as there will be no need for bowls in heaven; and verse 24: *"The nations will walk by its light, and the kings of the earth will bring their glory into it,"* which could refer to qualities from the Millennium period carried forward into the eternal realm (for no earthly kings or their glory will exist there).

Something similar happens with Revelation 22, where a reference is made that appears to apply to the Millennium rather that the eternal kingdom: *"On either side of the river* [of the water of life] *was the tree of life, bearing twelve kinds of fruit, yielding its fruit every month; and the leaves of the tree were for the healing of the nations"* (v. 2). There are Bible interpreters who contend that there will be no need for food in heaven, that time will not exist there, nor that any healing will be necessary for the nations, which in themselves will not exist there as such. Except that there will be no need for the healing of the nations in heaven (no illness, death, or conflicts there), the Scriptures do not say anything about other conditions in heaven, so the rest is presumed.

In the opinion of the author of this book, some of the apparent (and very limited) superimposition of concepts in Revelation 21 and 22 has to do with the fact that *the Millennium will be the precursor of Heaven on Earth*, ruled by Christ with righteousness and justice. Heavenly blessings bestowed upon the millennial saints will be carried over into eternity, when Christ will merge the millennium kingdom into the kingdom of Heaven, as noted. However, the final test and necessary purging of Millennium men upon the release of Satan and his revolt at the end of that period will necessarily create a one thousand year chasm between both kingdom. Notwithstanding, regarding the notion of eternity, please note the prophetic words in 2 Peter 3:8: *"But do not let this one fact escape your notice, beloved, that with the Lord one day is as a thousand years, and a thousand years like one day."*

Eternity

The author has often mentioned that if men were to profoundly and periodically reflect upon the scope and meaning of eternity and the never ending consequences of our related decisions on Earth, there would be far less sin in the world.

The Scriptures do not provide details about life in the eternal kingdom of God, although Millennial conditions seem to foreshadow them.

Kinship with God

> *Beloved, now we are the children of God, and it has not appeared as yet what we shall be. We know that, when He appears, we will be like Him, because we will see Him just as He is.*
>
> —1 John 3:2

At a time when world conditions have weakened family ties because of generational value gaps (especially spiritual ones), distance, income disparities, and a host of other reasons, it is very hard to image what the infinite blessing and privilege to become a member of the family of God will be like—and not just for a season but through eternity.

Fellowship with God

> *Behold, the tabernacle of God is among men, and He will dwell among them, and they shall be His people, and God Himself will be among them.*
> —REVELATION 21:3

Beyond kinship, what an extraordinary blessing it will be to have eternal fellowship with the Lord, which is something worth pursuing now while we are still on Earth.

Coheirs with Christ

> *The Spirit Himself testifies with our spirit that we are children of God, and if children, heirs also, heirs of God and fellow heirs with Christ.*
> —ROMANS 8:16–17

If and when you worry about financial and economic problems, just think for a moment on what it would like to become coheirs with Christ in a kingdom where money and richness will serve no purpose, nor generate any concern.

A Kingdom of Peace

> *And the peace of God, which surpasses all comprehension, shall guard your hearts and your minds in Christ Jesus.*
> —PHILIPPIANS 4:7

This affirmation from the apostle Paul transcends our time on Earth and applies to the eternal kingdom of God, for this world has never provided sustainable peace to anyone, and perfect peace outside Christ is actually unknown to men. Indeed, this is why the peace of God "surpasses all comprehension," and it represents the true gate to happiness.

A Kingdom of Virtue

> *Whatever is true, whatever is honorable, whatever is right, whatever is pure, whatever is lovely, whatever is of good repute, if there is any excellence and if anything is worthy of praise.*
> —PHILIPPIANS 4:8

> These will undoubtedly be prevalent conditions in heaven, because they pertain to our unchangeable God. As admonished by Paul and Timothy for us while we are on Earth, *"Let your mind dwell on these things"* (Phil. 4:8).

A Kingdom of Joy

"And these things we write, so that our joy may be made complete" (1 John 1:4), for the kingdom of God will bring unending joy to the redeemed of the Lord.

A Kingdom Without Trials

> *And He will wipe away every tear from their eyes; and there shall no longer be any death; there will no longer be any mourning, or crying, or pain; the first things have passed away.*
> —REVELATION 21:4

What a beautiful promise. What a contrast with this world!

A Kingdom of Glory

> *For momentary, light affliction is producing for us an eternal weight of glory far beyond all comparison, while we look not at the things which are seen, but at the things which are not seen; for the things which are seen are temporal, but the things which are not seen are eternal.*
> —2 Corinthians 4:17–18

May we be able to understand that God sees us from the vantage point of eternity and not despair when we are confronted by diverse trials, recognizing that these are allowed to build up our faith and strengthen our character.

Thus, it is our prayer *"that the God of our Lord Jesus Christ, the Father of glory, may give to you a spirit of wisdom and of revelation in the knowledge of Him. I pray that the eyes of your heart may be enlightened, so that you will know what is the hope of His calling, what are the riches of the glory of His inheritance in the saints, and what is the surpassing greatness of His power toward us who believe"* (Eph. 1:17–19). Amen.

Chapter 6
CONCLUSIONS AND ADMONISHMENTS

Conclusions

The following summary is meant to provide the reader with a succinct version of the present world crisis and its correlation with biblical prophesies discussed in depth throughout this book. Its purpose is to correlate current trends with fundamental truths provided by Bible texts as a foundation for the admonishments that will follow.

The author's sincere desire is to help the reader discern and deal with the critical issues posed by the latter-days and the end-time revelations. Apocalyptic scriptures are perhaps the most difficult ones to understand and discern, for several most important reasons.

Up to the forthcoming Tribulation period, we will have learned about a *redeeming God* extending unlimited love and unwavering loyalty to all mankind despite its sinful nature, its selfish and unfaithful ways, and their limited regard for the realm of the Spirit. Even though the Lord has warned that *"the gate is small and the way is narrow that leads to life, and there are few who find it"* (Matt. 7:14), many people have focused their expectations in the scriptures that affirm that He is patient and does not wish anyone to perish. However, their true intent is to come to the Lord only after they have enjoyed "life to its fullest," a dangerous proposition, because no one knows when our soul will be required of us (Luke 12:20).

There are also those who have heard His Word but not adhered to it, blinded by the distractions and appetites of the world, and have become ambivalent and uncommitted about His call, deluding themselves into a false sense of religiosity, regarding which the Lord has sentenced, *"So because you are lukewarm, neither hot nor cold, I will spit you out of My mouth"* (Rev. 3:16).

Thus, as we have moved scripturally forward into the Tribulation period, apocalyptic prophesies have also disclosed the *gravity and severity of the judgments of God*. These were addressed in ancient times as *"the great and awesome day of the Lord"* (Joel 2:31), and they are clearly portrayed as the most terrible time in world history.

Thus, the preceding paragraphs lead us to *the essential contrast between a God of love and the severity of His judgments*—no ambivalence, no uncertainty, no middle ground, no lukewarm position. The apostle Paul expressed it with profound clarity: *"Behold then the kindness and severity of God; to those who fell, severity, but to you, God's kindness, if you continue in His kindness"* (Rom. 11:22).

The fundamental purpose of this book is to highlight what is at stake: the eternal kingdom of God, or eternal damnation. The choice is ours, and the time is at hand. Even today, with wars and rumors of war and the degradation of men's values and behavior in every field of human activity, we are provided glimpses of what is to come.

On the World Crisis

After having read the first chapter of this book, it should be evident to the reader that the author considers that the present world crisis is far from over, despite a concerted effort by the leading nations to provide information to the contrary.

The political, economic, financial, and social policies of the leading governments are influenced by factors of power that transcend nations and international organizations, which in turn are manipulated by *"the world forces of this darkness"* (Eph. 6:12), something that for the most part leaders and experts, in their worldly pragmatism, have chosen to ignore.

It is clear that nations are dealing with the effects and not with the causes of the political, socio-economic, and financial crises, and for example, continue to promote consumption beyond the means of the people to prevent recession—all while governments themselves incur growing budget deficits and alarmingly increasing national debts. Bestselling authors John Mauldin and Jonathan Tepper, in their book *Endgame: The End of the Debt SuperCycle and How It Changes Everything*, write the following relative to the USA's debt:

> Debt is moving from consumer and household balance sheets to the government. While the debt supercycle was about the unsustainable rise of the debt in the private sector, endgame is the crisis we will see in the public sector debt. Real endgame is when governments begin to run into the limits of their ability to borrow money at today's low rates. Greece already has. Others will follow.[7]

Actually, the same is true for the most advanced nations.

Inflation is currently restrained by sluggish purchasing power conditions (including unemployment), and the controls levied on interest rates and on the prices of certain commodities. However, if monetary stimulus is abandoned in the future and interest rates are allowed again to become competitive, inflation could become a critical problem.

Virtual funds created via derivatives continue to threaten

the stability of world finances, and any disruption in its fragile and largely uncontrolled mechanisms, given its colossal monetary volume, could derail the international economic and financial systems, with devastating consequences.

So far governments have managed to control social and political reactions against their policies in various countries, some more successfully than others. However, as disposable income contracts, as high levels of unemployment remain, and as the consequences of recession, general mismanagement, and its impact on the quality of life of the populations become more apparent, this could rapidly get worse.

It is a statistical fact, as noted in the first chapter of this book, that super-state or socialist types of governments are becoming more prevalent among the nations. These states currently control an increasing share of their gross national products, along with regulatory body of norms that weighs heavily of the private sector. These policies can only lead to decreasing efficiency and productivity, as communist and socialist countries have evidenced in recent decades.

How can super-sized governments pretend to effectively lead the private sector when they cannot manage their own budgets? How can they speak of sustained, albeit moderate (or non-existent) economic growth, when this is at the expense of increasing national debts, mainly fed by money printing? The excellent book titled *This Time Is Different, Eight Centuries of Financial Follies*, written by Carmen H. Reinhart and Kenneth S. Rogoff is one of the best empirical investigations of financial crises ever published. It covers sixty-six countries over eight hundred years of history until the present. In it we read:

> The lesson of history, then, is that even as institutions and policy makers improve, there will always be the temptation to stretch the limits. Just as an individual can go bankrupt no matter how rich she starts out, a financial system can collapse under the pressure of greed, politics and profits no matter how well regulated it seems to be. Technology has changed, the height of humans has changed, and fashions have changed. Yet the ability of governments and investors to delude themselves, giving rise to periodic bouts of euphoria that usually ends up in tears, seems to have remained a constant.[8]

Thus, while it is true that history should teach us about tomorrow, it is also a fact that men forget about past errors and commit the same mistakes over and over again. Bible prophesies written thousands of years ago about these latter times also seem to be ignored by most, despite warnings and signs that could not be clearer.

Greediness and pride are the great inducements used by the forces of evil to bring the world into its present condition. As it has been stated in this book, the real objective of the forces of evil is to bring about a new world order under a centralized power to be usurped by the Antichrist during the forthcoming Tribulation period. Despite the deterrence brought about, thus far, by weapons of mass destruction, the increasing international economic and financial disarray might create enough political and social pressures on governments so as to increase the risk of regional conflicts or the reenactment of Cold War conditions.

What to do in the light of such a grim outlook? Seek counsel and protection from above, both for the short and the long term. Here are words of wisdom:

> *How blessed is the man who does not walk in the counsel of the wicked, Nor stands in the path of sinners, Nor sit in the seat of scoffers! But his delight is in the law of the Lord, And in His law he meditates day and night. He will be like a tree firmly planted by streams of water, Which yields its fruit in its season And its leaf does not wither; And in whatever he does, he prospers.*
>
> —PSALMS 1:1–3

On Spiritual Warnings

A warning from God always carries a blessing, but if unattended, it may lead us astray. For *"there is a way which seems right to a man, But its end is the way of death"* (Prov. 14:12).

Warnings become necessary because men are greedy, self-centered, egotistical, and selfish, and most often words of wisdom are unheeded or ignored. This is so because man's capacity to discern has been impaired by the distractions of the world and his spiritual vision clouded by the pursuit of material things and carnal desires. God is calling men today to move to higher grounds, for His thoughts and ways are higher than ours (Isa. 55), and He lovingly desires that we walk by His side in this treacherous world. While Christ has warned us that *"apart from Me you can do nothing"* (John 15:5), He has also reassured us that in Him we can do all things. A very fair proposition, indeed!

A warning should generate awareness, i.e., (a) an understanding of what is required to confront a threat, and (b) a disposition to act upon it. One is useless without the other. In these latter days as the church advances toward its Rapture from Earth to be spared from the Tribulation period that is looming in the horizon we are warned by

God, *"Be on the alert then, for you do not know the day nor the hour"* (Matt. 25:13).

On Spiritual Signs

The issue with spiritual signs is that they must be spiritually discerned, which means that men's perception and understanding of those signs—which combine spiritual thoughts with spiritual words—must originate from the Spirit of God, who Christ identified and sent to us as the one who will guide us into all truth. However, to the worldly man, with a carnal mind, the things of the Spirit are foolishness. He simply cannot understand them because they must be spiritually appraised and cannot be grasped by human knowledge alone.

Thus, ask for wisdom from God with faith, and He will give it to you; and not just for yourself but also for the unbelievers that He will put in your path. The Word says, *"Freely you received, freely give"* (Matt. 10:8).

Learn and proclaim the spiritual signs given by the Lord Jesus to His disciples, and your message to the stranded will be strengthened.

Tell them about the Lord Jesus Christ, whose coming and deeds were announced through thirty-seven direct and explicit prophesies, all fulfilled—irrefutable evidence of His deity and of the truthfulness of His Word.

Tell them that He is the way, the truth, and life and that no one goes to the Father but through Him;

Proclaim the good news: that anyone can be saved through faith in Christ Jesus. Do the work of a missionary:

- *Everywhere*, for where you are, that is your mission field (Africa and Latin America may sound very romantic, but it may not be for you).

- *In season and out of season*, and the Lord will guide you and tell you what to say.

- *Preaching with your example*, which is worth more than a thousand words.

- *Under prayer*, rightly dividing the Word of God in whatever you do (preaching, teaching, writing, testifying).

- Pray for the unsaved.

If one can do all those things, the Word says that *"he shall be called great in the kingdom of heaven"* (Matt. 5:19).

On External Signs

Many people say, "If God does this or that for me, then I will believe." Interestingly, the Lord Jesus actually accepted this challenge from the Jews while on Earth when He said, *"If I do not do the works of My Father, do not believe Me; but if I do them, though you do not believe Me, believe the works, so that you may know and understand that the Father is in Me, and I in the Father"* (John 10:37–38). Thus, while the Word says that men's faith without works is dead, the works of God to revive our faith must be accepted as a loving sign from Him.

For this reason prophetic, external signs given by God for these latter days can be directly compared in purpose with the works Christ did during His days on Earth: to make men believe what He has foretold us in His Word. While spiritual signs are given for spiritually discerning people, external signs are given for all men to behold and acknowledge. They are given in a clear progression:

1. First are those major signs that have already occurred and are evident to all (e.g., the return of the Jewish people to the Promised Land, the repossession of Jerusalem by Israel, the flourishing of Israel).

2. Second are those foretold events that are actually unfolding in our present days. Knowledge is rapidly increasing; there is a war raging on for the control of the mind of men; there is an evident surge of the confrontation between emotionality and spirituality, which influences our lives; further, there are external forces of evil that disguisedly (and increasingly) constrain freedom and promote the manipulation of fear aimed at influencing people's behavior. All this is prevalent in our days and continue to unfold right before our eyes.

These external signs have been addressed earlier in this book for your evaluation and edification. Please scrutinize the scriptural support provided therein; those prophecies were written thousands of years ago for this time in history. Compare that evidence from the Bible with what is going on at present. The correlation between prophecy and the fulfillment of the Word is, indeed, miraculous. This is a most important fact, because the world has already entered into a time of deception and confusion, a time which heralds the Great Tribulation period. The Scriptures warn:

> *Woe to those who call evil good, and good evil; Who substitute darkness for light and light for darkness; Who substitute bitter for sweet, and sweet for bitter! Woe to those who are wise in their own eyes And clever in their own sight! Woe to those who are heroes in drinking wine And valiant men in mixing strong drink; Who justify the wicked for a bribe, And take away the rights of the ones who are in the right!*
> —Isaiah 5:20–23

We must take notice that the signs, works, and miracles of God that we are allowed to read about, to witness, and even to participate in, along with the extraordinary blessing that they represent, do transfer a great deal of responsibility to us. Jesus was very explicit about it:

> *Then He began to denounce the cities in which most of His miracles were done, because they did not repent. "Woe to you, Chorazin! Woe to you, Bethsaida! For if the miracles had occurred in Tyre and Sidon which occurred in you, they would have repented long ago in sackcloth and ashes. Nevertheless I say to you, it shall be more tolerable for Tyre and Sidon in the day of judgment than for you."*
> —Matthew 11:20–22

On Latter-Days Events

As noted, the latter days in which we are presently living only foreshadow the far more serious and calamitous conditions that will emerge during the seven-year Great Tribulation period, also addressed as *"the day of the Lord's wrath"* (Zeph. 1:18).

However, you will recall that in line with the Lord's biblical promises, the true Church of God, that which has kept the Word of His perseverance, will be kept *"from the hour of testing, that hour which is about to come upon the whole world, to test those who dwell on the earth"* (Rev. 3:10). This holy church will be caught up in the air to be with Christ immediately after the resurrection of those that previously died in Christ. This event is commonly referred to as the Rapture, and it will occur at any moment prior to the forthcoming Tribulation period.

It is critical to understand that between now and the Rapture of the Body of Christ there is a unique window of opportunity for men to secure their salvation. Conversely, for those who disregard the Lord's warnings and proceed on into the Tribulation period, besides having to confront the worst and most horrendous period in world history, their eternal salvation may, for the most part, become possible only through martyrdom.

It is no less essential to understand that the option is not between enjoying the worldly pleasures at its fullest and then just simply dying, as some argue. What is at stake is eternal damnation, *"for if we go on sinning willfully after receiving the knowledge of the truth, there no longer remains a sacrifice for sins, but a terrifying expectation of judgment and the fury of a fire which will consume the adversaries"* (Heb. 10:26–27). There is no ambiguity about this. The Lord Jesus said it Himself, *"Do not marvel at this; for an hour is coming, in which all who are in the tombs will hear His voice, and will come forth; those who did the good deeds to a resurrection of life; those who committed the evil deeds to a resurrection of judgment"* (John 5:28–29).

Thus, this is the moment to search for the way, for we have been given the signs and directions to find. This is the time to secure the truth, for the Word has made it clear to all those who seek it, and the reward is eternal life in God's everlasting kingdom.

The removal of the constrainer from Earth—the Holy Spirit of God who indwells the true church of God, who leads the saints on to the knowledge of the truth and guides them on to the path of life—will take place along with the raptured church and prior to the Tribulation period. This will be necessary for the lawless one (the Antichrist) to be revealed during the seven-year dispensation period granted by God to the Antichrist and the false prophet under Satan's guidance and as a final test for those who will remain on earth during the Tribulation.

Indeed, for those who remain in the world, the absence of the Holy Spirit and His restraining power on the forces of evil, along with the disappearance of the true church and of the power vested in them by Christ over the forces of darkness, will bring about enormous confusion, the weakening of their faith, and of the fear of the Lord. Most will feel that they have been abandoned by God, when in reality it will be them who have separated themselves from Him. This infinite spiritual vacuum will be the precursor of the Tribulation period.

The Tribulation period will then begin on the earth, which will be populated by Jews and Gentiles who rejected the eternal salvation made possible by the vicarious offering of the Lord Jesus Christ at the cross. As commented, this will be a time like no other in history, shortened by the Lord for the sake of the elect, i.e., the remnant of Israel and the Tribulation saints. The conditions they will have to endure are difficult to describe and, in due course, will be hard for them to endure.

If self-deception and ignorance existed while the Holy Spirit and the church were on Earth, just imagine how it will be during the period of prevalence of the Antichrist and the false prophet, who will be empowered by Satan after having been cast down to Earth along with his lost angels. During the seven-year dispensation granted to them by God as a final test to those who remain on Earth, in addition to socio-economic and trade restrictions, this false trinity will be allowed to control all media, communications, and every and all activity of men, and without any resemblance of legal, ethical, moral, or human principles, nor, needless to say, of true spiritual values. Repression will be dictatorial and merciless.

Thus, during this period the worst of people will come to the surface. The preservation of oneself will become the rule, while love, family ties, friendship, and spiritual values will be put to the test. Conversely, the best of many men will also emerge, and the remnant of Israel and the Tribulation saints will live through heroic days and suffer persecution and death, as the early church did.

The mercy of the Lord will be manifest through the witness of the one hundred forty-four thousand Jewish preachers, who under God's protection will call all people to repentance and salvation. Israel will receive the visitation and testimony of the two witnesses, who will be killed and resurrected in the presence of many, and their testimony will save one-third of the Israelite nation (the remnant).

During the second half of the Tribulation period the wrath of God will be poured out upon the unsaved and the whole earth, and as we have already discussed, this will result in the devastation that the releasing of the seals and the trumpet and bowl judgments will bring about.

This series of apocalyptic events will culminate with the war of Armageddon, the last conflict to take place involving the Antichrist and the false prophet against not only Israel but God Himself. The insanity and absurdity of those attempting to confront God will be different for the various players:

- For the Antichrist and the false prophet, their expectations of prevailing upon Christ at His second coming will result from the blindness caused by pride, hatred, and the absolute—even though short-lived—dominion of the world attained by them. They will delude themselves that they will force the hand of God, being that so many people will be exposed to their utter destruction. But they have been judged already, and their fate is already sealed, i.e., to be thrown alive into the lake of fire.

- For all nations and peoples who will have received the mark of the Beast, this will be the result of the confusion and deception caused by the Antichrist's and the false prophet's domination of the world, their signs and wonders, the Antichrist's faked death and resurrection, and his apparently unchallenged desecration of the temple, impersonating God Himself. On the other hand, the absence of the Holy Spirit's wisdom and the living testimony of His church, which will no longer be on earth, will also influence their misjudgment. Most people will have developed an unrepentant heart against God because of the severity of the judgments to be confronted during the Tribulation, for which they will blame God.

- For Satan, after the obliteration of his forces at Armageddon, he will be locked by God's angel into the abyss for one thousand years during the millennial kingdom of Christ of Earth. After that time he will be released for a short while, causing a brief and final revolt that will be immediately crashed by Christ (the last cleansing of those on Earth). Satan will then be thrown down in to the lake of fire that never quenches, where the Antichrist and the false prophet will already be, along with all those who received the mark of the Beast.

This will finally put an end to Satan's rebellion both in Heaven and on Earth and forever close the struggle between good and evil. All other evildoers will then be resurrected (the second resurrection of damnation) and judged at the Great White Throne of Christ, according to their deeds.

The fulfillment of the Father's promise to put all enemies under the feet of Christ will lead to the creation of a New Heaven and a New Earth, finally enabling the merger of the millennial kingdom of Christ into the eternal kingdom of God for all eternity.

Admonishments

We Need God's Help

The Spirit of God has guided us through the scriptures scrutinized in this book to understand some of what is currently going on in these latter days. As our world is clouded by misinformation and deception, by emotions and confusion, how we translate this knowledge into wisdom and action is a personal challenge that we can only pursue with God's help. Faith in God is the confidence that He can and that He wishes to help us seek that which we desire according to His Word, even if we do not see it yet with our natural eyes and mind (Heb. 11:1).

The world advocates the opposite, that man has to have faith in himself, to become self-sufficient, to be smart, ambitious, and focused in his own interests and objectives to succeed in life. Spiritual thoughts and deeds are foolishness to him, for they have no spiritual discernment.

However, for those who are sincerely wrong, not correctly discerning the things of the world from the things of God, as was the condition of the apostle Paul when he was a Pharisee and a persecutor of Christians, the author believes that Lord will surely come to the rescue, for He sees the heart of men. That could be your case today, and the Lord says, *"Come now, and let us reason together"* (Isa. 1:18).

Do Not Be Proud

Pride that exalts oneself above all others is disrespect in the presence of God. Do not expect to be heard or receive anything from God having a proud attitude, for *"pride goes before destruction, And a haughty spirit before stumbling"* (Prov. 16:18). Rather, be *"gentle and humble in heart"* (Matt. 11:29), as the Lord exhorted us to be, and He will hear your prayer and guide your steps. Understanding God's infinite power and greatness truly helps us appreciate His blessings and to fear His wrath.

Open the Door of Your Heart

The Lord says, *"Behold, I stand at the door and knock; if anyone hears My voice and opens the door, I will come in to him and will dine with him, and he with Me"* (Rev. 3:20).

Notice that the Lord says that it is not only necessary to hear His voice, but to open the door as well. Clearly it is not enough to hear His Word, but one needs to act upon it, for faith without works is dead.

Reject Temptation

Let us consider what the essence of temptation is: an evil desire to do something contrary to the Word of God that is processed in the heart of men, originating from within or in response to external evil stimulus. It does not originate from the Lord, because He does not tempt anyone, nor can He be tempted (James 1:13). Thus, the purpose of temptation is to distract our attention away from God, to take our focus and attention from Christ, and this can occur in many and diverse ways. To some it is *"the love of money... a root for all sorts of evil"* (1 Tim. 6:10); to others is power, and for many it is carnal desire, *"for the mind set on the flesh is hostile toward God"* (Rom. 8:6). For this reason Christ warned us in a most clear way: *"For what will it profit a man if he gains the whole world and forfeits his soul?"* (Matt. 16:26).

Many will attempt to justify their conduct by claiming to be overcome by temptation. But this is not true, for the Lord has declared, *"God is faithful, who will not allow you to be tempted beyond what you are able, but with the temptation will provide the way of escape also, so that you will be able to endure it"* (1 Cor. 10:13). Thus, the Lord has given us a free will to make unprejudiced decisions, and by these we will be judged. Further, He has reassured us that although in the world we will have trials and tribulations, we should *"take courage; I have overcome the world"* (John 16:33).

Follow His Lead

As we have repeatedly mentioned in this book, the Lord Jesus Christ has solemnly told us, *"I am the way, and the truth, and the life; no one comes to the Father but through Me"* (John 14:6). This is the central verse of the Scriptures. This defines Christianity: to be a follower of *Jesus* (which means "God's salvation"), and *Christ* (which means "the anointed One").

It is imperative to believe that *He is the way* to God's eternal kingdom and that the directions are provided in the Bible, the perfect spiritual GPS.

He has said that *He is the truth*, the knowledge of which will set you free from sin, confusion, temptation, and the evilness of this world. The truth is the foundation of wisdom and of the knowledge of God.

It is essential to find *the life*, as those who are in Christ today have already passed from death unto life. For the Lord has said, *"My sheep hear my voice, and I know them, and they follow Me; and I give eternal life to them, and they will never perish"* (John 10:27–28).

Keep His Commandments

Many orthodox religious people pay lip service to God's commandments but deny them in their hearts and with their conduct. Others choose to add to the Scriptures doctrines of men that suffocate man's spirit: *"'Do not handle, do not taste, do not touch!' (which all refer to things destined to perish with use)—in accordance with the commandments and teachings of men?"* (Col. 2:21–22). But the Lord says about them, *"Their heart is far away from Me...in vain do they worship Me, Teaching as doctrines the precepts of men.... They are blind guides of the blind"* (Matt. 15:8–9; 14).

Instead, the Lord was clear as to which is the greatest commandment in the Law: *"'You shall love the Lord your God with all your heart, and with all your soul, and with all your mind'… The second is like it, 'You shall love your neighbor as yourself.' On these two commandments depend the whole Law and the Prophets'"* (Matt. 22:37, 39–40). These are the commandments that we should strive to follow and live by.

Talk to God

The emphasis here is on the word *talk*, which really means "to converse" or "to freely exchange views and thoughts." One talks, and the other one listens, as you talk to your father, your brother, or to a friend.

The Lord Jesus thought us *how not to pray* when He said not to be hypocritical about it, praying in the synagogues or street corners just to be seen by men. Instead, He said, pray privately to your Father, and He will repay you. When praying, *"do not use meaningless repetition, as the Gentiles do, for they suppose that they will be heard for their many words…for your Father knows what you need, before you ask Him"* (Matt. 6:7–8).

The Lord also thought us *how to pray*, with great sincerity, beauty, and respect:

- *Recognizing Him* with great reverence and consideration for Who He is: *"Our Father who is in heaven, Hallowed be Your name"* (Matt. 6:9)

- *Acknowledging His will* with devotion and meekness: *"Your kingdom come. Your will be done, On earth as it is in heaven"* (v. 10)

- *Presenting our petition,* asking for our needs rather than for our wants: *"Gives us this day our daily bread"* (v. 11)

- *Recognizing our commitment* with contrition, obedience and a merciful heart: *"And forgive our debts, as we also have forgiven our debtors"* (v. 12)

- *Requesting guidance:* *"And do not lead us into temptation, but deliver us from evil"* (v. 13), for He has promised that if we trust Him in our hearts and do not lean unto our own understanding but *"in all [our] ways acknowledge Him...He will make [our] paths straight"* (Prov. 3:6).

- *Giving glory:* "For Yours is the kingdom and the power and the glory, forever. Amen!" (Matt. 6:13). These are profound testimonial words of faith and praise to God that bless us and those who hear us.

The Lord also told us to *pray privately* in the intimacy of our personal relationship with Him. Not that privacy changes the protocol of respect and recognition due to Him when we are in His presence and make our plea known, but intimacy often tests the sincerity of our love and devotion for Him, as we express it in words and thoughts. Our prayers should not be just to petition something, either for ourselves or for others but also to express our gratitude to God for being our Father and our friend; our counselor and our fortress against evil; the source of everything that is true, honorable, right, pure, lovely, of good repute, excellent, and worthy of praise (Phil. 4:8).

Also, *pray through your deeds*. When you reach the point that your life is dedicated to God, your very existence becomes a living prayer, for in everything you do you recognize Him. Jesus said, *"Whoever wishes to become great among you shall be your servant"* (Matt. 20:26); and about helping others, He told us, *"To the extent that you did it to one of these brothers of Mine, even the least of them, you did it to Me"* (Matt. 25:40).

Have a Personal Relationship with God

When everything is said and done, what will remain is your personal and loving relationship with Him, which, once established, will last forever. That is the reason and purpose for which we were created.

The Bible; the churches, temples, and congregations; the priests, pastors, and teachers appointed by God and the angels commissioned to guard you; the books written and the words spoken by men of God—all that has been purposed by the Lord to guide you and to edify your relationship with Him.

No one can replace you, nor take your place. You were created by the Lord as a singular individual, and you have received from Him unique qualities. He has testified this to you in the fact that you have unique eyes and fingerprints by which you can be recognized, different from all other human beings.

While the Lord has clearly stated that all men have been borne equal, it is also a fact that we will not all die the same, for we have been given a free will, and we shall be judged according to our own words and deeds (Heb. 9:27).

A PERSONAL NOTE FROM THE AUTHOR

The writer wishes to thankfully acknowledge the guidance of the Holy Spirit in the writing of this book, noting that his role has been only that of a messenger.

His intention is to direct the blessings and warnings that stem from messianic prophecies in the Old and New Testament to all people: Christians, Jews, and men of all religious backgrounds who sincerely seek God as the time draws near.

God has presented the truth about what is to come in these latter times with unequivocal signs and warnings, but men must use their own free will to acknowledge it and act upon it. What is at stake is the most important decision that anyone will be called to adopt in his or her entire life. Its consequences are not limited to it but will determine where one will spend the rest of eternity. This is a most sobering thought and one to meditate on it while there is still time. *Selah!*

The author formally declares this book to be an offering to God and disclaims interest in any personal benefit that could be derived from its publication.

NOTES

1. *Webster's New World Dictionary of the American Language*, 2nd College Ed. (New York, NY: Simon and Schuster, 1980), s.v. "sign."
2. King James Version of the Bible, PTL Partner Edition (Nashville, TN: Thomas Nelson, Inc., 1975), s.v., "Prophecies of the Messiah Fulfilled in Jesus Christ."
3. T. A. Bryant, ed., *Today's Dictionary of the Bible* (Ada, MI: Bethany House Publishers, 1982).
4. James Gwartney, Robert Lawson, Joshua Hall, et al, *Economic Freedom of the World* (CATO Institute, 2012), accessed at http://www.cato.org/economic-freedom-world (December 15, 2013).
5. Stephen D. Renn, *Expository Dictionary of Bible Words* (Peabody, MA: Hendrickson Publishers, 2005), s.v., "plégê."
6. J. Dwight Pentecost, *Things to Come* (Grand Rapids, MI: Zondervan, 1965), 365.
7. John Mauldin and Jonathan Tepper, *Endgame: The End of the Debt SuperCycle and How It Changes Everything* (Indianapolis, IN: John Wiley and Sons Inc., 2011), 25.
8. Carmen H. Reinhart and Kenneth S. Rogoff, *This Time Is Different, Eight Centuries of Financial Follies* (Princeton, NJ: Princeton University Press, 2009), 291–292.

CONTACT THE AUTHOR

You may contact Dr. Hector Caram-Andruet at author.caram.andruet@gmail.com

More Books
to Edify & Inspire You

CREATION HOUSE HAS BEEN AN INDUSTRY LEADER FOR MORE THAN 40 YEARS WITH WORLDWIDE DISTRIBUTION AND A REPUTATION FOR QUALITY AND INTEGRITY.

THE NEW HOPE TIMES	THE DEATH SHROUD	Morphing Orlando into a World-Class City	DESTRUCTIVE VIOLENCE AGAINST MEN
WAYNE ABEL	AMY SANDERS	RANDALL JAMES	MILVERTON ADESANYA
978-1-62136-387-3	978-1-62136-392-7	978-1-62136-396-5	978-1-62136-666-9
$10.99 US	$16.99 US	$16.99 US	$13.99 US

Visit Your Local Bookstore
WWW.CREATIONHOUSE.COM

Retailers: Call 1-800-283-8494
WWW.CHARISMAHOUSEB2B.COM